PROJECT ACHIEVEMENT:

Reading

George D. Spache, Ph.D.
Spache Educational Consultants

Evelyn B. Spache, Ed.D.
Spache Educational Consultants

And the Scholastic Editors

D

 SCHOLASTIC INC.

THE PROJECT ACHIEVEMENT STAFF

Curriculum Consultants:
Leonore K. Itzkowitz,
Reading Specialist,
New Jersey Public Schools
Phyllis Anderson Wood,
Reading and English Teacher,
Westmoor High School,
Daly City, California

Editorial Director: Eleanor Angeles
Design: Taurins Design Associates
Revision Production Team:
Rosalie Shagwert Hayek, Suzanne
Sayegh Thomas
Revision Supervision:
ZIGG-LYN Publishing Concepts
and Services

Printed in the U.S.A.   7 8 9/8 0/9

Contents

Introduction 5

UNIT I
READING COMPREHENSION   7

Part 1   Details and Main Idea 8
Lessons 1–8 10–25
Taking Tests 26

Part 2   Inference 30
Lessons 1–12 32–56
Taking Tests 57

Part 3   Critical Reading 60
Lessons 1–7 62–75
Taking Tests 76

UNIT II
VOCABULARY   79

Part 1   Synonyms and Antonyms 80
Synonyms and Meaning 81
Lessons 1–5 84–94
Word Review 95
Antonyms and Meaning 96
Lessons 6–8 98–104
Word Review 105
Taking Tests 106

Part 2   Context Clues 110
Lessons 1–4 114–121
Word Review 122
Taking Tests 123

Part 3   Words with Several Meanings 126
Lessons 1–3 130–135
Word Review 136
Taking Tests 137

Part 4   Word Parts 138
Lessons 1–2 142–145
Taking Tests 146

UNIT III
STUDY SKILLS
147

Part 1 Visual Materials 148
Lesson 1 Reading a Street Map 150
Lesson 2 Reading a Road Map 152
Lesson 3 Reading a Product Map 154
Lesson 4 Getting Information from Maps 156
Lesson 5 Reading a Table 158
Lesson 6 Interpreting a Bar Graph 160
Lesson 7 Reading a Line Graph 162
Lesson 8 Reading a Complex Line Graph 164
Lesson 9 Understanding a Circle Graph 166
Lesson 10 Getting Information from Graphs 168
Taking Tests 170

Part 2 Reference Skills 174
Lesson 1 Using a Dictionary 176
Lesson 2 Using a Table of Contents
          and an Index 178
Lesson 3 Using the Card Catalog 180
Lesson 4 Using the *Readers' Guide*
          to Periodical Literature 182
Lesson 5 Using an Encyclopedia 184
Lesson 6 Using an Atlas 186
Lesson 7 Using an Almanac 188
Lesson 8 Using Newspapers and Magazines 190
Lesson 9 Choosing the Right Reference 192
Taking Tests 194

UNIT IV
TESTS
197

Test 1 Reading Comprehension 198
         Vocabulary 202
         Study Skills 205

Test 2 Reading Comprehension 208
         Vocabulary 212
         Study Skills 215

Vocabulary Glossary 218
Answer Key 221

Introduction

One benefit of being a good reader is to be able to score well on tests. Here are four different ways that you can improve your reading skills *and* your test-taking skills.

1. By understanding the details in a reading passage.

Here is part of a reading passage you will find in this book.

By 1982, China was supposed to have about one billion people. But the precise number of people was not known. The only way the government could find out was by taking a census. Previously, China had taken a census in 1964. At that time, the population was just over 723 million.

China spent more than $200 million to take its most recent census. A large proportion of that money was used to pay for 29 new computers. In China's earlier census, the total population was added on an abacus, an ancient wooden counting device. In 1982, the new computers did the counting more quickly and accurately.

Complete the sentence: Since 1964, China's population has ___.

2. By figuring out what difficult words mean.

The words under **A** are from the passage above. Use clues from the passage to help you match each word with its meaning under **B**.

A	B
precise	part
previously	exact
proportion	tool
device	earlier

An abacus.

Find two more ways to improve your reading and test-taking skills on the next page.

3. By using visual materials, such as graphs and charts.

Study the circle graph and answer the question below it.

WHERE THE WORLD'S POPULATION LIVES

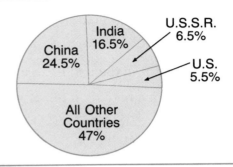

What share of the world's population lives in China?
    a. one tenth   c. about one half
    b. close to one fourth   d. nearly all

4. By recognizing the kinds of passages and questions that you will find on reading tests.

    Many inventions and discoveries were known to the Chinese well before they were known to people in other places. These include the compass, metal type, gunpowder, the kite, the wheelbarrow, and paper money. Early engineering feats in China include the Great Wall and the first Grand Canal, an 850-mile-long man-made waterway.

    Not every scientific or engineering effort in China turned out to be a success. For example, the Chinese had no better luck than anyone else in seeking a way to turn cheap metal into gold.

Choose the best answer.

This passage is mainly about China's ___.

    a. history   c. achievements
    b. Great Wall   d. engineers and scientists

Now you have practiced four kinds of reading and test-taking skills. You will find the same kinds of skills in the rest of this book.

Answers to exercises: **1.** increased or grown; **2.** precise — exact, previously — earlier, proportion — part, device — tool; **3.** b; **4.** c.

UNIT I
READING
COMPREHENSION

PART 1: *Details and Main Idea*   8

PART 2: *Inference*   30

PART 3: *Critical Reading*   60

Details and Main Idea

How many details can you find in this photo? The details can help you to describe the photo's main idea.

In a reading passage, the details are names, dates, facts, directions, and so on. The main idea is a short statement of what the passage is all about. A statement of the main idea will not always be found in the passage. Sometimes, you must put together the details in the passage to learn the main idea.

Almost all reading tests include questions about details and main ideas. The purpose of Part 1 is to help you learn how to answer questions about details and main ideas.

Find the details and the main idea in the following passage. Use the details to figure out the main idea. Read the passage and answer the questions below it.

Jet Alley

Jet planes flying overhead seem to be changing the weather in parts of the Midwest. Scientists say that the weather there is milder now than it was 15 to 20 years ago.

High-flying jets leave trails of white vapor behind them. During the day, these trails reflect sunlight away from the earth. At night, the vapor trails trap the earth's heat and keep it from escaping into space. So, there is less difference between daytime and nighttime temperatures than there used to be.

These changes in temperature are taking place beneath "jet alley" — a narrow piece of sky from northern Ohio to southern Missouri. As many as 9,000 planes fly through jet alley every day.

Choose the best answer for each question.

1. High-flying jets send out __.
   a. sunlight
   b. cold air
   c. vapor trails
   d. heat

2. Daytime and nighttime temperatures have become __.
   a. more alike   c. the same
   b. less alike   d. colder

3. What is the main idea of the passage?
   a. Jet planes fly into space.
   b. The weather in the Midwest is warm.
   c. Vapor trails trap the earth's heat.
   d. Jet planes can affect the weather.

Check your answers. You should have chosen **c** for 1, **a** for 2, and **d** for 3. If you missed Question 1 or 2, look back at the passage to find the correct details. If you missed Question 3, review the details in the passage to figure out the main idea.

Find the details and the main idea in the next passage. Then complete the questions that follow. Each question has only one correct answer.

The Pothole Problem

Each year, U.S. cities and towns spend millions of dollars to repair potholes, those deep holes in the road. Potholes are usually caused by heavy rain or snow. The holes get deeper when snow keeps melting and freezing.

The average pothole is 16 inches across and 5 inches deep. Potholes can bend the parts of a car or blow out a tire. They can cause serious traffic accidents.

Because of the danger, road crews fill the biggest potholes right away. But keeping up with potholes is a hard job. In big cities, potholes open up faster than workers can fill them.

A crew of three or four workers can fill a pothole in 12 minutes. There are several steps. First, pebbles and loose pieces of asphalt — a black, crumbly material — are raked out of the hole. Then, the sides of the hole are chopped straight with a special tool. The next step is to pour tar along the edge. The workers then shovel hot liquid asphalt into the hole. It takes about 100 pounds of it to fill an average-sized pothole. The asphalt is smoothed out, packed down, and pressed flat with a heavy metal roller. Finally, more tar is poured around the hole to seal it.

The effort to keep the streets smooth never ends because potholes never stay filled. Heavy traffic takes out some of the filling. Rain or snow may reopen a pothole. So, the crews return many times to fill the same potholes.

Choose the best answer for each question.

1. What happens to a pothole when snow melts and freezes?
   a. The pothole disappears.
   b. The pothole gets larger.
   c. The pothole is filled.
   d. The pothole freezes.

Check your answer. Read all the answer choices before you choose the best one. Look back at the passage if you need to. The correct detail is in the first paragraph. The answer is **b**.

2. What is the first step in filling a pothole?
   a. chopping the sides of the hole
   b. pouring tar
   c. clearing out pebbles
   d. pouring in hot asphalt

Check your answer. Find a series of steps in the fourth paragraph. Read the first step to check your answer. The right answer is **c**.

3. How much asphalt is needed to fill an average-sized pothole?
   a. 12 pounds   c. 50 pounds
   b. 16 pounds   d. 100 pounds

Check your answer. When there are several numbers in a passage, be sure to choose the one that relates to the question. The correct answer is **d**.

4. A pothole is sealed with ___.
   a. tar   c. water
   b. asphalt   d. a metal roller

Check your answer. Sealing the pothole is one step in filling it. Find the right detail in the fourth paragraph. The answer is **a**.

5. This passage is mainly about ___.
   a. how potholes are formed
   b. repairing potholes
   c. how asphalt is made
   d. the number of potholes in cities

Check your answer. Look back to review the details in the passage. What are most of the details about? Put together the details to decide on the main idea. The answer is **b**.

Find the details and decide on the main idea in the next passage.
Complete the questions, and then check your answers.

The Crowded Castle

   William Randolph Hearst was a wealthy newspaper publisher. He
used some of his riches to build a castle in San Simeon, California.
Hearst filled the castle with valuable works of art, including paintings,
furniture, and jewels from palaces in Europe. Some of the art works are
hundreds of years old.

   Hearst's castle is now an art museum. It is one of the most popular
tourist attractions in California. Nearly a million people visit the castle
each year. All those visitors are putting the art works in danger. The
problem is body heat.

   Art works must be kept at about the same temperature all the time.
Because of all the visitors, the temperature in the rooms of the castle is
always changing. The temperature goes up a few degrees when people
enter a room, and it drops again when they leave. At least 30 groups of
tourists visit San Simeon at a time, so people are constantly entering
and leaving rooms. Drafts from opening and closing doors also cause
some of the damage.

   Workers at San Simeon are taking several steps to save the art
treasures. They keep doors from being opened and closed more than
necessary. They inspect the art works often for signs of damage. Even
with this kind of care, about half a million dollars is spent each year to
repair paintings and furniture.

   The most important way of protecting the art works is to limit the size
of the crowds. About 200,000 visitors are turned away each year.

Choose the best answer for each question.

1. The art works at San Simeon are in danger because of ___.
   a. fingerprints
   b. rain
   c. body heat
   d. thieves

2. Which of the following is *not* given in the list of art works?
   a. paintings
   b. statues
   c. furniture
   d. jewels

3. What happens when many visitors enter a room in the museum at once?
   a. The room temperature rises.
   b. The room temperature drops.
   c. The carpet is worn out.
   d. The museum is closed.

4. How many people visit the museum each year?
   a. 200,000
   b. about half a million
   c. 30 groups
   d. almost a million

5. Which of these titles best describes the main idea of the passage?
   a. "The Life of William Randolph Hearst"
   b. "Visiting Hearst's Castle"
   c. "Jobs in Museums"
   d. "Treasures in Danger"

Check your answers.

Question 1: Without reading the passage, you might guess that several of the answer choices could be right. But you will find the correct detail in the second paragraph. The answer is **c**.

Question 2: Notice the word *not* in the question. You need to find out which details *are* in the passage to know which one is not. The correct answer is **b**.

Question 3: Check the passage to find the paragraph about changes in room temperature. It is the third paragraph. The answer is **a**.

Question 4: Several numbers are given in the passage, some in figures and some in words. Choose the right one. The answer is **d**.

Question 5: Review the details in the passage. Answer choice **b** is an important part of the passage, but it is not what the passage is mainly about. The right answer is **d**.

Look for the details and the main idea in each of the next passages.

Miracle Plant

Few people have heard of the winged bean. But the winged bean is starting to take off. Scientists believe that the winged bean will help end hunger in the poor countries of the world.

The bean plant was discovered in 1974. Scientists were looking for tropical plants that could be used as food. They found that the winged bean is highly nutritious. The plant can add important proteins, vitamins, and minerals to the diet. In poor countries, these things are often in short supply in people's diets.

The winged bean grows mainly in Southeast Asia. More than 800 kinds of winged beans have been counted in Thailand, Indonesia, and other countries. Unlike many vegetables, the winged bean grows well in places with heavy rains. It also grows well in poor soil and needs no fertilizer.

The winged bean looks like a pole bean. Its leafy stems can climb as high as 13 feet. Except for the stalk, every part of the plant can be eaten. The seed pods of the winged bean are like green beans. The pods are the most popular part of the plant. They can be eaten raw, or cooked in water, milk, or oil. Even the dried pods left after the seeds are removed are valuable as food. They can be fed to cattle.

The young seeds from the pods are like green peas. The mature seeds are used to make an oil that is rich in Vitamin E. The dried seeds can be made into a flour. Grinding and roasting the seeds can produce a drink like coffee.

The leaves of the winged-bean plant taste like spinach. When the flowers are cooked, they taste like mushrooms. The roots of the plant produce tubers like potatoes. Winged-bean tubers can be baked, boiled, fried, roasted, and even made into chips. No wonder scientists call the plant "a supermarket on a stalk."

The winged bean grows in more than 70 countries. There is a newsletter for scientists that is entirely about the bean plant. It is called "The Winged-Bean Flyer." The articles describe new uses for the wonderful winged bean.

Choose the best answer for each question.

1. In what part of the world does the winged bean mainly grow?
   a. in places with little rainfall
   b. in Southeast Asia
   c. in North America
   d. in poor soil

2. Why is the winged bean easy to grow?
   a. It needs heavy rain.
   b. It adds minerals to the diet.
   c. It can grow in poor soil.
   d. It is used to feed cattle.

3. Which part of the winged-bean plant cannot be eaten?
   a. the seeds
   b. the leaves
   c. the tubers
   d. the stalk

4. When cooked, the flowers of the winged bean taste like ___.
   a. spinach   c. mushrooms
   b. green peas   d. potatoes

5. This passage is mainly about ___.
   a. planting winged beans
   b. growing seeds and pods
   c. tropical plants
   d. winged beans as a food source

6. What is "The Winged-Bean Flyer"?
   a. a newsletter
   b. a pole bean
   c. a young bean plant
   d. a small plane

Snake on the Screen

Snakes, sharks, and giant insects seem to show up often in horror movies. Usually, these creatures are fake, or camera tricks are used to make a gentle creature seem horrible. But in a movie called *Venom*, the creature on the screen was every bit as dangerous as it looked. It was a real black mamba snake, the most dangerous snake in the world.

A snake's venom is the poison it injects into a victim when it bites. A black mamba bites without much warning. This snake can leap 10 feet in the air in a split second. Some snakes can be "milked" to remove the venom. The more dangerous the snake, however, the harder the job of milking it. The star of *Venom* kept all its deadly poison.

The black mamba snake was brought to the movie set from an animal farm in South Africa. A reptile trainer kept watch over the snake. The snake appeared in many scenes in the movie. It wriggled through the heating vents of a room. It jumped off shelves at people's necks. But no one was really in danger. The snake did all its acting behind a sheet of unbreakable glass. The trainer guided the snake toward the camera with a stick.

For close-up pictures of the snake's head, the trainer pushed the snake into a long, narrow tube. When the head came out one end, the trainer grabbed the tail. The snake looked directly into the camera, angry but still. Only the head would show on the screen.

The actors and the snake were never together in any scene while the movie was being made. Yet, in one scene, the snake appeared to bite a man. A movie trick made that scene possible. The trainer opened the black mamba's mouth and snagged its fangs on a man's coat. (The man was not wearing the coat.) Then the snake was pulled back. Later, this piece of film was run backward. Presto — a black mamba snake sank its fangs into the coat. This time, the man was wearing the coat. It was movie magic.

Choose the best answer for each question.

1. A snake's venom is its __.
   a. fangs
   b. trainer
   c. poison
   d. color

2. Which of the following does *not* describe a black mamba snake?
   a. It can jump 10 feet in a second.
   b. It bites without much warning.
   c. It is found in South Africa.
   d. It is tame.

3. *Milking* a snake means __.
   a. painting it white
   b. removing its venom
   c. collecting its milk
   d. grabbing its tail

4. How was the snake kept from hurting the people in the movie?
   a. Its venom was removed.
   b. It stayed behind glass.
   c. It was always kept in a tube.
   d. All of the above.

5. The snake became angry when its trainer __.
   a. grabbed its tail
   b. looked into the camera
   c. washed its skin
   d. jumped behind the glass

6. This passage is mainly about __.
   a. making horror movies
   b. using a dangerous snake in a movie
   c. raising a black mamba snake
   d. training animals to act in movies

7. The audience in a theater would *not* have seen the snake __.
   a. biting a man in a coat
   b. wriggling through a vent
   c. lying in a long tube
   d. jumping off shelves

The Uniform Factory

For more than 150 years, cadets at the U.S. Military Academy have paraded in their uniforms of "cadet gray." For nearly as long, tailors have stitched away at a factory right on the grounds of the academy at West Point, New York. The tailors turn stacks of gray cloth into uniforms. "The long gray line" of cadets in uniform is famous.

Seventy workers make about 4,000 uniforms a year for each new class of cadets. The uniforms are worn for four years.

Gray has been the color of the uniforms since 1816. The design has remained almost the same over the years, even when the first women cadets arrived in 1976. Skirts were added to the women's wardrobe of uniforms, but the only other changes were in size and shape. Women wear slacks when on parade.

At one time, the uniforms were made of heavy wool. Cadets wore the heavy uniforms in every season and for every activity — even gym class. Now a lighter-weight wool is used. Summer uniforms are made of cotton.

New cadets are measured for their uniforms on their first day at the academy. Stitching begins at the factory early in the morning. By afternoon, the cadets are wearing the main parts of their uniforms. Each cadet receives a wardrobe of many pieces: a long overcoat, a short overcoat, a full-dress coat, a heavy winter jacket, two dress coats, three pairs of heavy gray trousers, five pairs of lightweight gray trousers, and six pairs of white trousers. These items come from the academy's factory. Shirts, shoes, and hats are made by private companies.

Workers at the factory plan ahead to be ready for each new fall

class. In winter, they begin to prepare the uniforms for the next class of cadets. Tall stacks of wool are cut into shapes for jackets and coats. Other workers sew linings to sleeves and sleeves to jackets. The final touches of stripes and braids are then added.

During the school year, the factory workers make repairs on the uniforms. They may also change a uniform slightly to fit the changing shape or size of a cadet. Some workers keep busy adding stripes or other decorations to show a cadet's new class or rank.

Choose the best answer for each question.

1. The *long gray line* refers to the ___.
   a. line of cadets in gray uniforms
   b. gray line on a cadet's coat
   c. line of workers at the factory
   d. stripe on a pair of trousers

2. Which of these materials is used for summer uniforms?
   a. heavy wool
   b. silk
   c. light wool
   d. cotton

3. A cadet receives most of the uniform quickly because ___.
   a. the factory workers stay overtime
   b. part of the work is done months ahead
   c. the uniform lasts for four years
   d. no repairs are needed

4. Most of the details in the passage are about ___.
   a. a student's life at West Point
   b. making uniforms for cadets
   c. choosing a color for the uniforms
   d. repairing a uniform

5. Which of the following are *not* made at the uniform factory?
   a. jackets
   b. trousers
   c. overcoats
   d. shoes

6. Which step comes last in sewing a uniform?
   a. attaching sleeves to jackets
   b. cutting wool into patterns
   c. adding stripes and braids
   d. sewing linings to sleeves

The Town of Many Earthquakes

The small town of Moodus, Connecticut, is a quiet place. It is quiet if you don't count the noise from earthquakes.

For several hundred years, the town of Moodus has had an unusual number of earthquakes. There have been as many as six or seven earthquakes in a single day.

The quakes are usually tiny. They cause rumbling noises that last about 30 seconds. There is often a boom and a slight tremble of the earth. People in Moodus compare the noises to the sound of thunder or truck traffic.

Sometimes the earthquakes bounce beds, rattle windows, and shake dishes. One earthquake in 1791 did more serious damage, however. It knocked over many homes in Moodus.

Scientists believe that earthquakes take place along fault lines. These are deep cracks in the earth. But the cause of the Moodus earthquakes remains a mystery because no fault lines have been found in Moodus.

In the 1600's, the Wangunk Indians called this area Machimoodus, meaning "place of many noises." The Indians believed that the noises came from their god of evil, Hobomoko. They claimed that Hobomoko became angry when the English settlers did not worship him. So he began to thunder loudly and shake the earth.

Hobomoko was supposed to have lived under a small mountain in Moodus. Strangely enough, scientists now believe that the center of the earthquakes is at that same mountain.

In the 1700's, a doctor came all the way from England to try to solve the mystery of the earthquakes. He blamed the quakes on a glowing rock that he had found at the foot of the mountain. While the doctor was sailing home to England with the rock, his ship sank. Legends say that the rock still sends out a bright glow from the ocean floor.

In those early years, no records were kept of the number of earthquakes. Equipment for recording the earthquakes was not installed until 1979. The equipment showed that there were many more earthquakes than anyone had realized. There were 500 earthquakes in just one three-month period of 1981.

Choose the best answer for each question.

1. How was the earthquake in 1791 different from others in Moodus?
   a. It lasted longer than the others.
   b. It caused more thunder.
   c. It caused more damage.
   d. It started along a fault line.

2. The town of Moodus got its name from ___.
   a. an Indian name for the area
   b. the name of a god of evil
   c. an Indian word for *earthquake*
   d. the word *moody*

3. What is a fault line?
   a. a slight tremble of the earth
   b. a deep crack in the earth
   c. part of a mountain
   d. a piece of equipment for studying earthquakes

4. In the 1700's, an English doctor blamed the earthquakes on ___.
   a. Hobomoko
   b. traffic noises
   c. a glowing rock
   d. scientists

5. Why couldn't the earthquakes be counted before 1979?
   a. There were too many to count.
   b. Scientists could not decide which ones to count.
   c. Fault lines were found in 1979.
   d. Equipment to do so had not yet been installed.

6. This passage is mainly about ___.
   a. the causes of earthquakes
   b. the history of earthquakes in one town
   c. the old houses in Moodus
   d. an Indian village in the 1600's

Search Dogs

Search dogs are trained to find missing people. Using only its sense of smell, a single dog can search an area eight times faster than a search team of 20 people.

A search begins when the dog receives the scent from an article that the missing person has handled. The dog then sets to work following the scent.

Besides a good sense of smell, search dogs must have other special qualities. They must be able to learn quickly. They must be tough enough to withstand severe weather. Searches often take place in snow and bitter cold. Indoor pets don't have the thick, tough coats that are needed.

In the United States, search dogs are usually German shepherds or bloodhounds. German shepherds are especially useful in finding people after sudden emergencies, such as floods or earthquakes. Police use them to help find criminals, too. The dogs are smart and take orders well.

Bloodhounds are also used in police work. They have often followed a criminal's scent from the scene of the crime to a hiding place. Bloodhounds can "point out" a burglar in a large group of people. Bloodhounds are the best dogs to use for night searches. They have very poor eyesight, so they are able to concentrate fully on the scent.

Dogs cannot be used in every search. First, there aren't enough trained dogs to go around. The dogs may have to be flown to a place from hundreds of miles away. By the time they arrive, the scent may be too old for them to pick up.

In a very small area, search dogs are not usually needed. By the time a search dog is flown in, a search team could easily have found the missing person.

In some searches, weather conditions may not be right for a search dog. A scent is especially strong in damp weather. A slight wind also helps because it spreads the scent to a larger area. Then the dog can pick up the scent from farther away. But strong winds, heavy rains, and even hot weather can cause a scent to disappear.

For these reasons, dogs are used in only one out of every four searches. But when they are used, they prove their value. Search dogs have done some things that seemed impossible. Some dogs have tracked people across rivers. Others have followed a scent for 100 miles. A dog once found a person still alive under 14 feet of snow. There had been a snowslide on a mountain.

Choose the best answer for each question.

1. Which of these senses does a search dog rely on the most?
   a. taste
   b. touch
   c. smell
   d. sight

2. Which of the following weather conditions would cause a scent to die out?
   a. a slight wind
   b. dampness
   c. strong heat
   d. light snow

3. Which of these titles best describes the main idea of the passage?
   a. "How Dogs Are Used in Searches"
   b. "Training a Search Dog"
   c. "Bloodhounds in Police Work"
   d. "Following a Trail in Snow"

4. How are different kinds of search dogs alike?
   a. They all have sharp eyesight.
   b. They all can follow a scent for 100 miles.
   c. They are all bloodhounds.
   d. They all have thick coats.

5. A bloodhound's poor eyesight helps this dog to __.
   a. see better in the dark
   b. focus on the scent
   c. catch a burglar
   d. track missing people across a river

6. Which of these can search a small area best?
   a. bloodhounds
   b. a team of search dogs
   c. a team of people
   d. German shepherds

Down the Track

The start is the most important moment in Funny Car racing. There is only one-half second between the amber warning light and the green starting light. The drivers must make their starts between these two lights. They cannot wait for the green light before starting. There is a saying in drag racing that "if you see the green, you've lost the race."

At the same time, the drivers cannot start too early. A light beam crosses the starting line. If the nose of the Funny Car touches this light beam before the green light goes on, then the driver "red-lights." That means that a red light goes on to show that the car has fouled. The driver is out of the race. The other driver becomes the winner, if his car can make it to the end of the strip.

Therefore, the drivers must judge exactly the split second to start on the amber light and still not trigger the red foul light. It is here at the start that a drag race is often won or lost.

In the race, the drivers rev up their engines. The two Funny Cars leap away from the starting line. They are headed for a beam that crosses the track exactly 1,320 feet down the strip — one-quarter mile.

The fans leap to their feet as one car pulls slightly ahead of the other. The fans don't dare blink, for they could miss a vital part of a race that is over before they can count slowly to six.

The cars reach speeds of up to 245 miles per hour, but the race is not decided by speed alone. It is possible for the faster car to lose the race. A car's tires can slip at the start. Or a driver can be slow to start. Then, even if that car has a higher speed, the lost second — or split second — at the beginning will permit the slower car to cross the finish line first.

Choose the best answer for each question.

1. According to the passage, the winner of a Funny Car race is often determined ___.
   a. at the start of a race
   b. at the green light
   c. when a race ends
   d. halfway down the track

2. A driver red-lights by ___.
   a. turning on the headlights
   b. crossing the finish line early
   c. starting too soon
   d. stopping on the starting line

3. A split second is ___.
   a. one second exactly
   b. part of a second
   c. more than one second
   d. half a minute

4. The winning car is the one that reaches the finish line ___.
   a. at a higher speed
   b. in six seconds
   c. in the fewest number of seconds
   d. before the green light

5. This passage is mainly about ___.
   a. how to build a Funny Car
   b. the dangers of drag racing
   c. the champion Funny Car driver
   d. the start of a Funny Car race

6. Which of these is *not* given in the passage?
   a. the length of the track
   b. the length of a Funny Car
   c. the top speed of Funny Cars
   d. the color of the warning light

Find details and the main idea in each reading passage on the next four pages. Read the test tips before you read each passage. Put your answers to the questions on your answer sheet.

Test Tips: If you are not sure of an answer, look back at the passage. Some details will help you, even if the exact words are not there.

A new kind of camera has changed the way all cameras and film will be made in the future. The tiny camera was introduced in 1982. It uses film discs instead of rolls of film. It is possible that, one day, rolls of film will be a thing of the past.

The new camera has helped the average picture-taker snap better photos than were possible just a few years ago. The new camera advances the film and focuses itself. It also has a flash that turns itself on when needed.

The film disc is thin, flat, and round. Each film disc has 15 fingernail-sized pieces of color film. These tiny pieces of film are arranged in a circle on the edge of the disc. One piece of film is used for each picture. After a picture is taken, a tiny motor automatically turns the disc to the next piece of film.

Because the film disc is thin, the camera is, too. It weighs only six-and-one-half ounces, and is five inches long and less than one inch wide.

The Eastman Kodak Company made the new camera. Kodak is also working on equipment that will make it possible to show the pictures from the disc camera on a television screen.

---

1. Which of the following is the best title for the passage?
   a. "From Film Rolls to Discs"
   b. "How To Take Pictures"
   c. "Using a Flash"
   d. "The History of Cameras"

2. Which of these is *not* automatic in the new camera?
   a. advancing the film
   b. focusing
   c. turning on the flash
   d. loading the camera

3. Why is the disc camera thin?
   a. The camera folds up.
   b. The film disc takes up very little space.
   c. The camera is the size of a fingernail.
   d. The film disc is round.

4. What is one benefit of the disc camera?
   a. easy loading
   b. low cost
   c. pictures of better quality
   d. free film

Test Tips: Watch for main idea questions that ask you to choose a title for a passage. Most reading passages on tests have no titles.

If you have ever tried to keep a few spiders in a jar, you may have made an interesting discovery. In a few days, you may have only one spider. Many spiders are cannibals! Hungry spiders eat anything they are able to catch, including other spiders.

A spider has a very small mouth and does not actually "eat" its victim. Instead, it first sucks out the body juices from its victim's body. Then fluids from the spider are injected into the victim's body. These fluids turn the victim's tissues into juices that can also be eaten by the spider. Later, the hollow body of the victim is cast aside.

You may wish to study spiders as they capture or feed on their prey. You can keep many kinds of spiders in small, clear plastic containers with soft plastic caps. Pierce the caps for air. Be sure to keep only one spider in each container. Keep the containers in a cool place. If the spiders are not fed for a week, many of them will attack small live creatures that are placed in their containers.

Flies, caterpillars, or other spiders can serve as food. However, large ants and members of the wasp family may frighten the spider.

---

5. Which of the following is the best title for the passage?
   a. "Pet Spiders"
   b. "Animals That Eat One Another"
   c. "The Eating Habits of Spiders"
   d. "Catching Spiders"

6. How are spiders *cannibals*?
   a. They eat plastic containers.
   b. They eat other spiders.
   c. They inject fluid.
   d. They are always hungry.

7. Which of the following might frighten a spider?
   a. caterpillars   c. big spiders
   b. flies   d. large ants

8. In "eating" a victim, which of these does a spider do last?
   a. suck out juices
   b. inject fluids
   c. toss the body aside
   d. catch another spider

9. The best way to encourage spiders in containers to eat is to ___.
   a. fill the container with water
   b. keep the spiders hungry for a week
   c. remove the lid from the container
   d. feed the spiders a little each day

Test Tips: Try each answer choice with the question before you choose the best one.

Lead is used in many products. For example, it is in matches, dyes, some food cans, and leaded gasoline. Gasoline fumes send lead into the air. Surprisingly, lead pencils do not contain any lead at all. It is important to know about lead because lead can poison us. Even small amounts of lead in the body can cause lead poisoning.

Paint peeling from old buildings is often a source of lead. Small children who chew on paint chips may suffer from lead poisoning. Eating just a few flakes a day of paint containing lead can cause lead poisoning. Crumbling paint that turns to dust can also be a source of lead poisoning — even for those who don't chew on paint chips.

Layers of paint on the walls of many houses built before 1940 may have a high lead content. Most modern indoor paint does not contain lead, but outdoor paint may.

A simple blood test can detect lead poisoning. Children who live in old houses should be tested regularly. If they are found to have lead in their bodies, they can be treated with medicines that remove it.

Children with lead poisoning should be treated immediately. And the *source* of lead poisoning should be found and removed.

---

10. Paint with lead is often found in __.
    a. older houses
    b. houses built in the 1970's
    c. cars
    d. food cans

11. Which of the following contains no lead?
    a. gasoline   c. pencils
    b. paint   d. cans

12. What method is used to detect lead poisoning?
    a. a skin test
    b. an eye test
    c. a blood test
    d. a breathing test

13. Which of these would increase the amount of lead in the body?
    a. eating paint chips
    b. breathing dust from crumbling paint
    c. breathing gasoline fumes
    d. all of the above

14. Which of these is the best title for the passage?
    a. "Painting Old Houses"
    b. "The Main Causes of Lead Poisoning"
    c. "Medicines for Lead Poisoning"
    d. "The Manufacture of Lead"

Test Tips: Some reading tests have passages with words missing. If you understand the passage, you will know the missing words. Six words are missing from the passage on this page. First read the entire passage to learn the main idea, and keep the main idea in mind. Then choose a detail from the words below to complete each blank.

A group of apartments in Massachusetts is making daily 15 easier for the handicapped. The apartments are the first of their kind in the United States. They have been designed to meet the needs of people with 16 kinds of handicaps. Some of the residents are blind, some are in wheelchairs, and some have only one arm.

In the kitchens, the 17 of the shelves or counters can be changed. People in wheelchairs need low shelves, for example. The ovens open from the side and have pull-out counters beneath them. That makes it easier to take food from an oven and place it on the counter immediately. There are also pull-out work boards with cut-out spaces for bowls. The bowls are held firmly in place.

Everything in the apartments is easy to reach. Switches for lights, fans, and alarms are placed 18 . Electrical outlets can be reached from a sitting position. Windows are easily opened with the flip of a bar. The windows are extra-large and low for people who must spend a lot of time in bed.

Bathrooms are especially dangerous places for handicapped people. The bathrooms in the apartments are safer than ordinary bathrooms. There are showers instead of slippery 19 . The showers have wide openings for wheelchairs and a fold-out seat. Each bathroom has an alarm.

The new apartments have shown that safe homes can be built for handicapped people. Someday all new homes may be designed so that handicapped people can live in them as 20 as anyone else can.

15. a. eating   c. climbing
      b. living   d. swimming

16. a. different   c. slow
      b. new   d. poor

17. a. color   c. height
      b. weight   d. paint

18. a. outside   c. high
      b. quietly   d. low

19. a. floors   c. soap
      b. bathtubs   d. shelves

20. a. long   c. easily
      b. quickly   d. smart

What are the feelings of the people in this photo? The details in the photo can help you figure out a likely answer. The parts you see can help you to make an inference about what you don't see.

Making an inference in your reading means finding the meaning when it is not actually stated. Reading materials contain a lot of details. You won't always have to remember all the details, but you will need to understand what they mean. One way to do that is to decide how the details relate to one another.

On reading tests, many questions ask for answers that are not stated in the passage. The purpose of Part 2 is to help you learn how to answer those kinds of questions.

The questions with the next selection ask for inferences. Use the details in the selection to figure out the answers to the questions.

Stranded Whales

Whales are marine mammals — air-breathing animals that live in the sea. Sometimes a whale gets onto a beach or in shallow water and is stuck there. Nobody knows for sure why marine animals get stranded.

Scientists have found that most stranded animals are ill. One theory is that when a whale is sick, it might swim into shallow water. Then it could stay near the surface to breathe.

Most stranded whales die shortly after stranding. It is almost impossible to move a large whale safely. Also, a very large amount of food and medicine is needed to try to save a whale.

Choose the best answer for each question.

1. How can air-breathing animals live in the sea?
   a. They come up to the surface to breathe.
   b. They breathe through their mouths.
   c. They breathe only once an hour.
   d. They get air at the bottom of the sea.

2. Whales probably get stranded on a beach after they ___.
   a. look for food
   b. follow a boat
   c. swim into shallow water
   d. save a swimmer

3. The main reason that whales cannot be moved safely is probably because of their ___.
   a. sharp tails
   b. size and weight
   c. illness
   d. slippery skin

Check your answers. You should have chosen **a** for 1, **c** for 2, and **b** for 3. If you missed any of the questions, find details in the passage that will help you figure out the answers. The word *probably* in Questions 2 and 3 is a sign that the correct answer choices are not stated in the passage. You will have to make inferences, using the details given.

LESSON 1

Read the following selection. Then answer the questions by using details in the selection. Each question has only one correct answer.

Robots for the Home?

Robots are a success in factory work. They paint cars, drill airplane wings, and spray chemicals, for example. A factory robot is simply a box with an arm attached. Most robots do a certain job over and over again. There were 4,000 robots in U.S. factories in 1982, and the number is growing.

You might think that robots would be as useful in a home as they are in a factory. Why couldn't a robot do everyday chores in a home — wash the dishes, sweep the floors, take out the garbage?

Most scientists believe that robots for the home will be practical only in the distant future. First of all, a home robot would cost anywhere from $15,000 to $100,000. And even if everyone could afford one, a home is not the best place for a robot. Robots can't climb stairs, for example, and they would be too heavy to carry. Also, robots can't change their work place easily. Rooms in a home are different sizes. A robot designed to work in a large room might bounce off the walls in a smaller room.

Most home chores are much too complicated for a robot, scientists point out. They doubt whether a robot would ever be able to wash the dishes without breaking them.

A few companies have made a kind of home robot. In 1982, a department store advertised a robot that could walk the dog, water plants, and take out the garbage. This robot was controlled by radio, like a model airplane. It was more like an expensive toy than a true robot. A true robot is run by a built-in computer.

Choose the best answer for each question.

1. In the future, robots in U.S. factories are likely to be ___.
a. more like people   c. more widely used
b. out of work   d. more expensive

Check your answer. The word *likely* in the question means that you will have to make an inference by using details in the selection. The first paragraph explains that the number of robots in factories is growing. So, the correct answer must be **c**.

2. Most robots seem to work best by ___.
a. moving in circles   c. climbing stairs
b. staying in one place d. watering plants

Check your answer. Most robots stay in one place to do a certain job over and over again. The answer is **b**.

3. This selection is mainly about ___.
a. robots for the home
b. robots in factories
c. robots in movies
d. robots that are operated by radio

Check your answer. It takes more than a few details to make a main idea. Answer choices **b** and **d** are small parts of the selection, and **c** is not mentioned at all. The right answer is **a**.

4. Which of these would today's robots be *least* likely to do?
a. spray paint   c. wash clothes
b. drill holes   d. tighten bolts

Check your answer. Answer choices **a**, **b**, and **d** are similar to the factory jobs that are listed in the selection. The right answer is **c**.

5. The first robots in homes are likely to be used in ___.
a. a bedroom and a kitchen
b. only one room
c. only a small room
d. only a large room

Check your answer. Use the details in the third paragraph to choose an answer. The details suggest that a robot works best in one room, no matter the size. The answer is **b**.

LESSON 2

Read the next selection. Use the details in the selection to answer all the questions. Then check your answers.

Chris' Walking Footlight

Have you ever tried to walk, run or work in the dark? A sixteen-year-old boy from New Jersey did. He decided that a little "walking footlight" for the road would be a good idea.

One day Chris Urban pulled his sneakers apart. He found air spaces in them. These spaces were between the cloth and the rubber part of the shoe. He thought that these air spaces would be a good place to put wires. He could attach the wires to batteries. The batteries could then be attached to small lights.

Chris was a fan of James Bond movies and the TV series "Mission Impossible." He enjoyed watching his film heroes use all kinds of exciting gadgets to catch criminals. It was these small mechanical devices he had seen in the movies that inspired Chris to invent his "light up" sneakers.

After performing several experiments, Chris finally got his sneakers to work. Whenever the wearer stepped down on the sole, the red lights would go on and flash. When the person picked his foot up, the lights would go off.

He entered his sneakers in the Duracell Scholarship Competition in 1985. His sneakers won second place in the contest. He also won a $3,000 scholarship.

These sneakers are more than a fun item. They provide an extra measure of safety for people who walk or run at night. They also make bike riders more visible in the dark. People who fight fires or do rescue work at night could be seen more easily.

Companies are looking into marketing Chris's sneakers. Since Americans are doing more outdoor activities at night, the light-up sneakers will make a real contribution to safety.

Choose the best answer for each question.

1. In which part of the sneakers was the best location for wires?
   a. in the heel
   b. near the laces
   c. the air spaces
   d. under the sole

2. The article suggests that the "light up" sneakers were inspired by ___.
   a. films
   b. advertisements
   c. experiments
   d. a fireman

3. What does "performing several experiments" mean?
   a. acting something out
   b. trying to make things
   c. watching something work
   d. trying or testing something many times

4. Which of these titles tells the selection's main idea?
   a. "Bicycle Riding at Night"
   b. "Sneakers for Safety"
   c. "Selling an Idea"
   d. "Entering Contests"

5. People who wear the sneakers that light up could probably ___.
   a. play better in ballgames
   b. ride bicycles in the country
   c. work more safely in the dark
   d. have to weigh under 200 pounds

Check your answers.

Question 1: Look for details about parts of the sneaker. Find the detail that gives the answer to the question. The answer is **c**.

Question 2: Details in the third paragraph clearly suggest a connection between the movies and Chris's invention. The answer is **a**.

Question 3: Clues in the passage suggest that performing an experiment means to keep trying or testing something to prove that it works. The right answer is **d**.

Question 4: Review the details in the entire selection. What are most of the details about? Put the details together to decide on the main idea. The answer is **b**.

Question 5: Details in the passage suggest that people who work or play in the dark would benefit most from the sneakers. The answer is **c**.

LESSON 3

Read the next selections and answer the questions. Use the details to make inferences.

Taking Command

When a boat runs into trouble near the shore or out at sea, a Coast Guard cutter is usually called to the rescue. Mary Jane Wixsom has taken part in many rescues. She is the first woman to be given command of a Coast Guard cutter. Her cutter has a crew of 14 men.

Lieutenant Wixsom's cutter is the *Cape Strait*. It is called out on as many as 25 "search and rescue" missions a year. When there are no calls for help, the cutter patrols New York harbor and the waters along the New Jersey coast.

Like all Coast Guard cutters, the *Cape Strait* enforces the laws of the sea. The crew may stop any boat that comes into or out of a harbor. They make sure a boat has a proper license. They look for life jackets and fire extinguishers. They search boats that may be carrying dangerous or illegal supplies.

Mary Jane Wixsom took command of the *Cape Strait* in March 1982. By then she had already had more adventures than most young women of 23. Starting in 1980, she was a boarding officer on a cutter that was patrolling the Yucatan Channel, a narrow body of water near the Gulf of Mexico. The channel was a main drug-smuggling route from South America to the southeastern United States. Coast Guard cutters were on the alert for boats carrying drugs.

Lieutenant Wixsom's cutter chased one boat for more than six hours before it was stopped. She and four others boarded the boat after dark

and searched it. They found 17 tons (34,000 pounds) of drugs. The Coast Guard crew arrested the 11 men on board and towed their boat into port.

Mary Jane Wixsom has won five medals for her achievements in the Coast Guard. The hardest achievement may have been completing the years of training at the Coast Guard Academy. "At first I only stayed because I hated it so much," she said. "I couldn't let it defeat me."

Choose the best answer for each question.

1. In the passage, the word *cutter* refers to a ___.
   a. boat in trouble
   b. large knife
   c. Coast Guard boat
   d. piece of equipment on a boat

2. The crew of a cutter probably spends most of its time ___.
   a. searching boats
   b. patrolling coastal waters
   c. arresting people
   d. attending school

3. Details in the passage suggest that all boats ___.
   a. must follow safety regulations
   b. are stopped by the Coast Guard
   c. have drugs on board
   d. are commanded by women

4. A boarding officer on a cutter probably ___.
   a. drives the cutter
   b. brings the cutter into port
   c. takes charge of searches on boats
   d. makes sure the crew is on board

5. This passage is mainly about ___.
   a. a career in the Coast Guard
   b. a search and rescue mission
   c. how to drive a cutter
   d. the commander of the *Cape Strait*

6. Details in the passage give the impression that Mary Jane Wixsom is ___.
   a. angry
   b. determined
   c. old-fashioned
   d. frail

Music to Their Ears

Stereo sets with headphones started appearing in 1979. The headphones were on the ears of walkers, joggers, bicycle riders, and drivers. By the end of 1982, more than 10 million people around the world owned the tiny machines.

The owner of Sony, a Japanese company, invented the sets. He wanted to be able to listen to hi-fi music while playing tennis. Many companies now produce models. Some sets play cassette tapes; others play AM or FM radio. A few even combine all three. The lightweight sets allow people to listen to their favorite music at its loudest, without bothering anyone else.

As the sets grew more popular, some people began to worry about their use. One worry is about the dangers of an accident on the street. A person wearing headphones cannot always hear the horn of a car or a warning shout. That fact has led some states to take action. By the end of 1982, nine states had passed laws that banned the use of headphones by drivers. Some towns and cities also wanted to keep pedestrians and bicycle riders from using headphones in the street.

Another worry is that the headphone sets could damage a listener's hearing. Scientists in Japan studied the hearing of 150 high school students who used headphones regularly. They found that eight students had a hearing loss. These eight students listened to their stereo headphones an average of six hours a day. But when they stopped using the headphones, their hearing returned to normal.

Choose the best answer for each question.

1. The main reason that 10 million people bought the headphones is probably that the sets ___.
   a. are not expensive
   b. can be used almost anywhere
   c. keep out noises
   d. play cassette tapes

2. In some states, it is against the law to wear headphones while ___.
   a. bicycling
   b. jogging
   c. driving
   d. playing music

3. Headphones would probably be accepted in a library because ___.
   a. libraries are crowded
   b. no one else could hear the music
   c. the headphones are small
   d. students use libraries

4. The passage gives the impression that headphones ___.
   a. always cause a hearing loss
   b. are hard to use
   c. are a waste of money
   d. should be used with caution

5. Why were high school students probably used in a study in Japan?
   a. The students are young.
   b. The headphones are popular with students.
   c. All students own headphones.
   d. Students have better hearing than anyone else.

6. What would scientists probably suggest to owners of headphones?
   a. Stop using them from time to time.
   b. Play the music at a high volume.
   c. Clean the headphones regularly.
   d. Stay out of cars.

The Long Count

On July 1, 1982, five million people started off with bundles of questionnaires to visit all parts of China. The five million people were census-takers. Their job was to count every person in China, the country with the biggest population.

China is supposed to have about one billion people — one fourth of the world's population. But the exact number of people in China was not known. The only way the government could find out was by taking a census.

Most countries of the world count their populations every 10 years. The last U.S. census was in 1980, and there will be another in 1990. The last census in China was in 1964. At that time, the population was just over 723 million.

China spent more than $200 million to take the 1982 census. A large part of that amount was used to pay for 29 new computers. In China's 1964 census, the total population was added on an abacus, an ancient wood-bead counting tool. In 1982, China could count its huge population quickly and accurately with the new computers.

A census of one billion people had to be carefully planned. The five million census-takers traveled on foot or on bicycles in the crowded cities of eastern China. They opened an office in every neighborhood. People were supposed to report to an office near their homes. Some census-takers spent months in the mountains and prairies of western China, searching for people to count. The final total was 1,031,882,551 people.

The census-takers not only counted the people; they also collected other information. How many men and how many women were living in China? What were the ages of the people? How long had they attended school? Answers to these questions and others will help China's government plan for the future.

China's new computers will continue to be used long after all the numbers from the census were added up. Thousands of men and women are being trained to run and repair the computers. The computers will help China in its drive to become more modern.

Choose the best answer for each question.

1. Taking a census means __.
   a. counting the people in China
   b. taking people on a tour of a country
   c. counting all the people in any country
   d. moving people from cities to the mountains

2. Where do most people in China live?
   a. in the eastern cities
   b. on the prairies
   c. on the southern coast
   d. in the north

3. According to the selection, the new computers will help the census-takers to __.
   a. find people in the cities
   b. count the number of people without error
   c. spend less money on the census
   d. divide the country into neighborhoods

4. What is an abacus?
   a. a new computer
   b. a census-taker
   c. a small city
   d. a simple counting tool

5. Details in the selection suggest that China has few __.
   a. automobiles   c. bicycles
   b. people   d. neighborhoods

6. The selection is mainly about __.
   a. China's large population
   b. computers in China
   c. China's most recent census
   d. planning China's future

7. How will China's new computers help the country in the future?
   a. The population will increase.
   b. New jobs will be created.
   c. Every household will have a computer.
   d. A census will be taken every year.

LESSON 6

Super Sculpture

In 1961, an art show called "The Store" opened in New York City. Bacon, sides of beef, and roasts hung from the ceiling. There were cases filled with gooey-looking cakes, pies, and ice-cream sodas. But all this "food" was made out of plaster and dripping with bright paint.

The plaster food was created by a Swedish-American artist named Claes Oldenburg. Oldenburg's objects were a new kind of art called "pop" art. This name was chosen because the objects were a reminder of popular American customs.

One of Oldenburg's first popular sculptures was a giant hamburger. It was a "soft" sculpture, one of many he worked on. He used a large piece of heavy cloth and cut four circles from it. He sewed these circles together and filled them with foam rubber. He painted the parts to look like a real hamburger on a roll, with a slice of pickle.

Is a giant hamburger a work of art? Many people didn't think so. But Oldenburg had a serious purpose in using ordinary things in his sculpture. He wanted people to see familiar objects in a new way. The sculptures were humorous. They showed that art could be fun. Certainly, his sculptures have always attracted a lot of attention.

Some of Oldenburg's large sculptures stand outdoors in several U.S. cities. There is a red steel baseball bat in Chicago. It rests on its handle and extends 100 feet into the air. In Philadelphia, a concrete clothespin stands 45 feet high on a main street. The biggest lipstick ever made is in an outdoor square at a college in New Haven.

Oldenburg's sculptures are built only after he tries out an idea in many different ways. He makes drawings and scale models of an object. Sometimes he makes thousands of tiny sculptures out of cardboard. When all the experimenting is finished, a familiar object will become a work of art.

Choose the best answer for each question.

1. The word *pop* in *pop art* is a nickname for ___.
   a. population   c. popular
   b. popcorn   d. Popeye

2. Oldenburg seems to get his ideas for sculptures from ___.
   a. newspapers and magazines
   b. common objects
   c. foam-rubber circles
   d. old paintings

3. How does Oldenburg show that he is serious about his work?
   a. He experiments carefully before building a sculpture.
   b. He asks people not to laugh at his work.
   c. He gives all his sculptures to colleges.
   d. He copies the styles of other artists.

4. A soft sculpture is partly made of ___.
   a. steel   c. stone
   b. cloth   d. wood

5. A likely subject for Oldenburg's art would be ___.
   a. a toothbrush   c. a dog
   b. a tree   d. an athlete

6. This passage is mainly about ___.
   a. giant hamburgers
   b. changes in pop art
   c. Oldenburg's scale models
   d. sculptures of ordinary objects

Saving the Falcons

The peregrine falcon is a rare and lovely bird. It is usually found on cliffs and mountain peaks. Now these falcons may have a new home — on the roofs and ledges of city skyscrapers.

In recent years, the long-winged birds have become endangered. Many have been killed by hunters or by other birds. Others have died from pesticides sprayed into the air. To keep all the falcons from dying out, scientists began to raise a few baby falcons in protected places. But after the babies were raised, where would they go?

They couldn't return to the old places. Instead, they were brought to cities. Since the early 1970's, scientists have released many falcons in cities in the United States and Canada.

Cities are good places for falcons for several reasons. First, the falcons like to nest on the tops of buildings. The city skyline is remarkably like the mountain ranges where the falcons usually live. Second, the sparrows and pigeons that live in cities are easy prey for falcons. Finally, the great horned owl, the falcon's natural enemy, is hardly ever seen in a city.

Falcons set free in cities usually do well, but they do face certain dangers. Some birds are killed when they crash into buildings. Many new skyscrapers have a shiny surface like a mirror. The birds may be confused by their own reflection. Other falcons die when they eat small birds that are sick.

Even with these dangers, many falcons will survive. Scientists have been working on a plan to turn another 600 falcons loose in cities and the countryside.

Choose the best answer for each question.

1. The falcons were taken to cities because their old homes were ___.
   a. unsafe
   b. dirty
   c. hot and damp
   d. overcrowded

2. According to the selection, what do falcons in cities eat?
   a. great horned owls
   b. sparrows and pigeons
   c. green leaves
   d. peanuts and garbage

3. The city skyline probably reminds falcons of ___.
   a. the U.S. and Canada
   b. their mountain homes
   c. roofs and ledges
   d. shiny mirrors

4. This selection is mainly about ___.
   a. hunting for falcons
   b. raising falcons in the countryside
   c. taking falcons to cities
   d. building new skyscrapers

5. In the mountains, falcons may be attacked by ___.
   a. scientists
   b. sparrows
   c. pigeons
   d. great horned owls

6. If the scientists' plan works, what will happen to the falcons?
   a. They will all die out.
   b. Six hundred falcons will be left.
   c. Many will survive.
   d. All falcons will live in cities.

LESSON 8

High Flyers

It was a great moment in circus history. At first, Miguel Vazquez and his brother Juan did not believe they had done it. They had performed the first quadruple somersault on the trapeze. The "quad" is four backward spins in midair. It is one of the hardest of all trapeze feats.

An acrobat named Lena Jordan did the first triple somersault back in 1897. Ever since then, trapeze artists have tried again and again to do one more flip. None had succeeded until 17-year-old Miguel Vazquez and his 32-year-old brother did it on July 10, 1982. The audience was astounded.

Miguel and Juan come from a family of Mexican circus performers. Miguel is the flyer, the one who does the somersaults. Juan is his catcher. When Miguel was only 13, he performed his first triple somersault. Only a few trapeze artists have done the triple. Miguel did the triple so well that Juan urged him to try for the quad. After constant practice, Miguel was ready.

Although a safety net hangs below the performers, the quad is full of dangers. If something goes wrong, both brothers could land on their necks or heads.

The quad is swift. The flyer spins through the air at 75 miles per

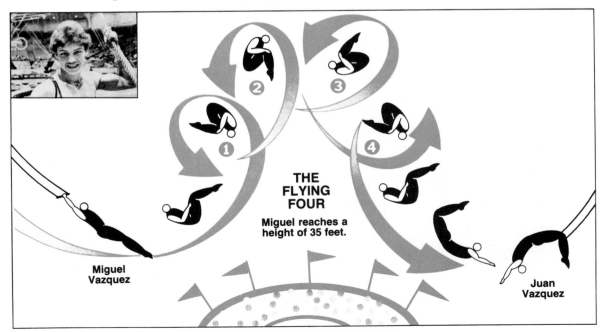

THE
FLYING
FOUR

Miguel reaches a height of 35 feet.

Miguel
Vazquez

Juan
Vazquez

hour. At that speed, there is nothing that Miguel can do to correct a mistake. It is up to his brother to catch his hands as he spins out of his fourth somersault. If the timing is wrong, the catcher may miss the flyer by a split second. They may even collide.

But Miguel and Juan didn't miss. Their hands connected and held.

Choose the best answer for each question.

1. What feat did Miguel Vazquez perform on July 10, 1982?
   a. He did a triple somersault.
   b. He did a quadruple somersault.
   c. He started performing on the trapeze.
   d. He caught his brother in midair.

2. How many spins are in a triple somersault?
   a. two   c. four
   b. three   d. five

3. Why is the quadruple somersault so dangerous?
   a. The flyer travels at a high speed.
   b. There is no safety net.
   c. The performers get dizzy.
   d. There is no catcher.

4. How has Juan been important to Miguel's success?
   a. He dared Miguel to do harder tricks.
   b. He taught Miguel everything he knows.
   c. He encouraged Miguel.
   d. He took Miguel to the circus.

5. Miguel probably wanted to do the quad because ___.
   a. it looked like fun
   b. it is dangerous
   c. nobody else had done it
   d. his brother dared him to do it

6. Most circus acrobats have probably done ___.
   a. a double somersault
   b. a triple somersault
   c. a quadruple somersault
   d. all of the above

LESSON 9

Eel Fishing Comes Back

An eel is a fish so long and thin that it looks like a snake. The flesh of an eel makes good food. One of the best places to catch eels is Lake Champlain, in northwestern Vermont.

For hundreds of years, the Abenaki Indians fished for eels in Lake Champlain. They called July "the month of the eel." In July, the eels were fat and easy to catch. Eel was an important part of their diet, along with deer, moose, and beaver.

In time, the Abenaki tribe grew smaller. Its members began to lose interest in catching eels. Then state laws in Vermont made fishing for eels illegal.

In 1982, those laws were changed. Now many of the 1,200 Abenaki tribe members are making a living by fishing for eels once again. They sell the live eels to fish sellers in Boston for about a dollar a pound. That is higher than the usual price for eel because the ones from Lake Champlain are high in quality and free of pollution.

Many restaurants in northern Vermont have been adding eel to their menus and giving out eel recipes. Eel has never been a popular dish in the United States, however. A part of the catch is flown to Europe, where eels are a special treat — like steak in the U.S.

The boom in eel fishing came at the right time for the Abenaki tribe. More than half the tribe members had been out of work. The Abenaki use a modern method of catching eels. It is called electro-fishing.

A short burst of electricity is shot into the water from the fishing boats. The electricity stuns the eels, stopping them from moving. They are then scooped out of the water with nets attached to poles 10 feet long. Electro-fishing is done at night, in shallow water. Arc lights make the scene almost as bright as day.

Choose the best answer for each question.

1. July was called the month of the eel because ___.
   a. restaurants sold many eels in July
   b. laws about eel fishing were changed then
   c. most eels were born at that time
   d. eels were fat and easy to catch then

2. What happens to an eel when a burst of electricity stuns it?
   a. It is killed.   c. It can't swim away.
   b. It glows in the dark.   d. It jumps into a net.

3. Why do the eels from Lake Champlain bring a good price?
   a. They are harder to catch.
   b. They are longer than other eels.
   c. They are better-tasting than other eels.
   d. They are very scarce.

4. Why did the Abenaki choose eel fishing to make a living?
   a. Laws in Vermont forced them to do so.
   b. Eel fishing is an old custom among the Abenaki.
   c. Eels have become popular as food.
   d. Lake Champlain has a new supply of eels.

5. What was one result of the new laws about eel fishing?
   a. Prices for eels went down.
   b. More jobs were created.
   c. Lake waters became cleaner.
   d. Other Indian tribes moved to Vermont.

6. This passage is mainly about __.
   a. fishing for eel in Lake Champlain
   b. the history of the Abenaki tribe
   c. fish sellers in Boston
   d. the story of Lake Champlain

LESSON 10

Rocky Mountain High Wind

A harsh wind blows along the eastern foothills of the Rocky Mountains each winter. The wind has a special name. It is called a *chinook*. At times, it has the force and fury of a hurricane.

The season for the chinook lasts about five months. January is usually the worst month. That is when the wind sometimes blows at about 130 miles per hour.

The chinook is especially strong in Boulder, a city of 80,000 people in Colorado. That is partly because Boulder lies at the very foot of the Rockies. The wind is born high in the mountains when winter storms move east across the continent. The storms pass over the mountaintops, and the wind comes crashing down the eastern slope. As it moves, it increases in speed and temperature. During one bad windstorm in Boulder, the temperature rose nearly 40 degrees in a few hours.

The chinook spares no city in its path. Telephone poles are snapped in two. Roofs are torn from houses. The people in Boulder have seen such damage often. A new law there requires that builders use "hurricane bolts" to tie down roofs of new houses. Builders also test small models of houses and stores in wind tunnels. This is to make sure that doors won't blow off if they are opened into a gust of wind.

The chinook has more than enough force to turn windmills. That became certain after scientists tried an experiment. They set up a station for generating power by windmills in the path of the chinook. A windstorm blew by with such force that one of the windmills was knocked over.

Choose the best answer for each question.

1. In what direction does a chinook travel?
 a. from east to west
 b. from west to east
 c. from north to south
 d. from south to north

2. The chinook is very strong in Boulder because of the city's ___.
 a. beauty
 b. size
 c. climate
 d. location

3. Details in the passage suggest that the chinook is a ___.
  a. warm wind
  b. cool wind
  c. frosty wind
  d. light wind

4. Hurricane bolts are probably ___.
  a. shaped like a lightning bolt
  b. strong and heavy
  c. easy to bend
  d. full of water

5. Scientists experimented to see if a chinook could ___.
  a. knock over a windmill
  b. open a door
  c. snap a telephone pole
  d. generate power

6. Small models of houses can suggest the effect of wind on ___.
  a. old houses
  b. wind tunnels
  c. full-sized houses
  d. hurricane bolts

7. Most of the details in the passage are about ___.
  a. summers in Boulder
  b. new laws for builders
  c. a strong wind in the Rockies
  d. a chinook that powers windmills

LESSON 11

The Birth of a Bridge

There is an old saying: "Every bridge demands a life." When the Brooklyn Bridge was built in New York, the first life lost was that of the chief engineer, John Roebling.

John Roebling had designed several other bridges, but the Brooklyn Bridge was his greatest challenge. Work began in 1869. In the first month of building, Roebling's foot was crushed by loose beams. He soon died of an infection.

John's son, Washington Roebling, took over as chief engineer. He had worked closely with his father on four bridges, and was prepared to carry out his father's plans.

The plans called for a suspension bridge across the East River, from Brooklyn to Manhattan. Stone towers, weighing 70,000 tons each, would stand at each end of the bridge. Four steel cables would be strung between the towers to support the roadway. It was the first use of steel in bridge-building.

The most dangerous part of building the bridge was sinking the caissons in the river. These were two strong wooden boxes, each half the size of a city block. They would rest on the bottom of the river and support the twin towers.

Workers inside the caissons used explosives to blast away sand and mud. As they did so, the caissons sank lower. The men often stayed underwater too long or came to the surface too quickly. Many suffered from "caisson disease." Severe pains in the chest and limbs were common. Some men were crippled and never recovered. Others died.

In June 1870, the caisson on the Manhattan side was 106 feet under water, 30 feet from the river bottom. Roebling worried about the danger

and ordered the sinking to stop. To this day, the caisson rests on sand rather than rock.

Roebling himself suffered from caisson disease. It nearly killed him. He insisted on staying in the caissons to inspect every detail of the work. He became too ill to leave his bedroom but continued to direct the work from his apartment near the bridge.

It took three years to build just the caissons. The entire bridge was finally finished in May 1883. The first passenger on the bridge was Emily Roebling, Washington's wife. She rode across in a horse-drawn carriage, carrying a rooster for good luck.

Choose the best answer for each question.

1. What is meant by the saying "Every bridge demands a life"?
  a. A bridge will save lives.
  b. Every bridge changes the lives of those who cross it.
  c. Building a bridge demands years of effort.
  d. Someone is bound to die while a bridge is being built.

2. What were the steel cables used for?
  a. to support the towers   c. to sink the caissons
  b. to support the roadway   d. to remove sand and mud

3. According to the passage, one sign of caisson disease was ___.
  a. a foot infection   c. sharp chest pains
  b. a feeling of dizziness d. swollen limbs

4. Washington Roebling probably stopped the sinking of a caisson because ___.
  a. he was too ill to continue working
  b. he ran out of explosives
  c. the caisson had already reached bottom
  d. he wanted to prevent injuries

5. The passage gives the impression that Washington Roebling was ___.
  a. stubborn   c. nervous
  b. confused   d. bored

6. The details in the passage are mainly about ___.
  a. the life of Washington Roebling
  b. how a bridge was built
  c. the dangers of caisson disease
  d. the opening of the Brooklyn Bridge

Amelia Earhart, a famous pilot in the 1930's, describes the start of her flight from Honolulu to California. Questions are on pages 55–56.

The Take-Off

Early on the morning of January 11, 1935, the clouds began to gather over Honolulu. By 11 o'clock, a tropical downpour was in full force. The military airport from which I planned to take off had no hard-surface runways. I knew that if I left that afternoon, I should have to lift my heavy load from very soggy ground.

At one o'clock, conditions were no better. At 3:30, the rain definitely let up and it looked as if the clouds might lift. So I went down to the hangar in which my plane was kept to look over the situation. I found the field soaked. However, I asked the men to get the plane out, put in the few remaining gallons of gas the tank would hold, and warm up the motor. I wished the plane to be ready in every detail.

The plane was a craft to delight the eye. Its wings and body were painted red with gold stripes down the side. It may have seemed a little too fancy on the ground but I am sure it looked lovely against one of those white clouds. It was a closed plane. I drive a closed car and fly a closed plane. I don't like to be mussed up. Also, a closed plane makes the pilot less tired.

My plane, a Vega, normally carried six passengers and the pilot. The

six passenger seats had been replaced by large fuel tanks carrying 520 gallons of gasoline. There are no service stations between Honolulu and California!

My cockpit was a very cozy little cubbyhole. I sat on a cushion just large enough for me. On the right-hand side of the seat was a large black box, the radio. The dials were on top so I could reach them easily. On the left was a large compass and two pump handles. The pumps enabled me to change fuel from one set of tanks to the other.

After I asked the men to warm up the motor, I went over to the Weather Bureau for a final check. I found that if I did not leave that afternoon, I would be held by storms coming in over the Pacific.

So, at about 4:30, I returned to the plane. The motor purred sweetly. I crawled into the cockpit and tested it myself. It sounded perfect. I told the men to take away the blocks in front of the wheels. I turned the plane and headed for the take-off pathway. Glancing to the left, I noticed three fire engines drawn up in front of the hangars, and one ambulance. The take-off with a heavy fuel load is the most dangerous moment because of the chance of fire if anything goes wrong. But please do not compare such a take-off with those of ordinary everyday flying. It is no more fair to compare the two than to compare automobile racing and safe automobile driving!

I put the plane in take-off position and looked down the long pathway ahead of me. I pushed the throttle ahead. The Vega started to move and gather speed. I felt the tail come up. The plane got lighter and lighter on the wheels. After rolling about 2,000 feet, a large bump on the field threw the plane completely off the ground. I pushed the throttle ahead to the farthest notch and gave her all the power I had. The plane started to settle, then caught — and we were off.

I have often been asked what I think about at the moment of take-off. Of course, no pilot sits and feels his pulse as he flies. He has to be part of the machine. If he thinks of anything but the task in hand, then trouble is probably just around the corner.

Choose the best answer for each question.

1. The runways at the airport in Honolulu were probably ___.
   a. paved with concrete
   b. made of dirt
   c. covered with plastic
   d. painted with stripes

2. Why did the author seem to prefer a closed plane?
  a. It kept out the wind.
  b. It looked colorful.
  c. It moved as smoothly as a car.
  d. It could carry heavy weights.

3. What is the passage mainly about?
  a. a rainy day in Honolulu
  b. a pilot's feelings about flying
  c. preparing for take-off in a small plane
  d. loading a plane with fuel

4. What were the weather conditions at the time of take-off?
  a. A tropical downpour was soaking the field.
  b. A storm was moving near the airport.
  c. The rain had definitely let up.
  d. White clouds were covering the sky.

5. Why was the author's plane carrying extra fuel?
  a. The plane was delivering fuel to California.
  b. The plane had no gas tank.
  c. Some fuel might have leaked out.
  d. A long flight was planned.

6. According to the author, the most dangerous part of flying is ___.
  a. landing on soggy ground
  b. getting the radio to work
  c. taking off with a heavy fuel load
  d. taking off into a storm

7. Which word best describes the pilot's attitude during the take-off?
  a. fearful
  b. confident
  c. gleeful
  d. uneasy

8. The author believed that trouble occurs when a pilot ___.
  a. loses the directions
  b. takes unnecessary chances
  c. fails to concentrate
  d. checks the plane too many times

TAKING TESTS

Practice making inferences about each reading selection on the next three pages. Read the test tips before you read each selection. Put your answers to the questions on your answer sheet.

Test Tips: On a test, answer all the questions you are sure of first. Put a mark beside the ones you skipped. Then go back to those.

Are drive-in movie theaters disappearing? Drive-in movies were a success in the 1950's and 1960's. The car was "king" and gasoline was cheap. Theaters advertised "$1 a carload."

In the 1970's, however, things began to change. There was an oil shortage, and the price of gasoline went up. People took fewer unnecessary trips. The popularity of drive-ins began to fade. By 1984, there were only about 3,000 drive-in theaters in the United States, mostly in the West and the South.

Changes in the value of land also helped to put many drive-ins out of business. The theaters had been built on cheap open land, outside of towns and cities. As the suburbs spread out into the country, the land became more valuable than the theaters. Many theaters and the land they stood on were put up for sale. Hotels, shopping centers, and office buildings replaced the old drive-ins.

Some theaters gave way to indoor theaters with as many as 12 screens. The indoor theaters can remain open year round, while the season for many drive-ins is only from May to September.

---

1. The passage is mainly about ___.
   a. drive-in movies of the 1950's
   b. why indoor theaters replaced drive-ins
   c. bargain prices for movies
   d. the closing of drive-ins

2. What is meant by the phrase *the car was king*?
   a. Only rich people drove cars.
   b. Driving was very popular.
   c. Cars were more important than people.
   d. Car owners paid only a dollar for a tank of gasoline.

3. The total number of drive-ins will probably continue to ___.
   a. increase
   b. decrease
   c. increase in the South
   d. remain the same

4. Drive-ins are more likely to remain in places where ___.
   a. the population is growing slowly
   b. the land has a high value
   c. gasoline is going up in price
   d. shopping centers are expanding

Test Tips: Many tests contain poems. Use details in the poems to figure out the meanings of the poems. Sometimes the lines are numbered to help you answer questions. Read the entire poem first.

Concrete Trap

1 The fox at midnight in the city square
2 knows there's a way, but knows not which it is,
3 a path that leads to fields and woods and lair,
4 leaves underfoot, earth and the stirring air.
5 Bewildered stands the fox, too many streets
6 lead off too many ways, yet there is one
7 leads to the woods and to tomorrow's sun.
8 Under street lamps, between the straight house walls,
9 hard, geometric, baffling nose and eyes,
10 escape is there for him to recognize.
11 Bewildered stands the fox, questing the way,
12 and in the yards the dogs begin to bay.

Elizabeth Coatsworth

5. What does the title "Concrete Trap" mean?
   a. The fox has been caught in a hunter's trap.
   b. The path from the city is paved with concrete.
   c. The fox is trapped in a city of concrete buildings.
   d. The woods are a trap at night.

6. Why can't the fox find the path to the woods?
   a. The street lights have gone out.
   b. It is past midnight.
   c. The dogs are in the way.
   d. The city has too many streets.

7. In *Lines 5 and 11*, what does the word *bewildered* mean?
   a. excited   c. content
   b. confused   d. frightened

8. In *Line 9*, what do the words *hard* and *geometric* refer to?
   a. the fox's nose and eyes
   b. the city's buildings
   c. the street lamps
   d. a path that leads to fields

9. What has happened to the fox at the end of the poem?
   a. He is still in the city square.
   b. He is following every path.
   c. He is on the path to the woods.
   d. He is fighting with the dogs.

Test Tips: As you read the passage, decide on a word that would probably fit in each blank. Then see if one of the answer choices in each group below matches your choice.

The French have built a train that can travel up to 236 miles per hour. It is called the TGV. The letters stand for "train à grande vitesse," or train of great speed. It is the _10_ passenger train in Europe.

The train's first run was from Paris to Lyon. The distance _11_ the two cities is 265 miles. Ordinarily, the trip takes almost four hours. It took the TGV only two-and-a-half hours.

The French have spent more than a billion _12_ on their new trains. The high-speed trains require special smooth tracks. Each train is about 600 feet long. There are no breaks between the cars, and each car is soundproof. There is an engine at each end of the train. The train is so fast and powerful that it can _13_ climb steep hills.

The trains are powered by electricity. The TGV uses only a little more energy than regular trains. It has a streamlined _14_ to cut the force of the wind.

The TGV moves too fast for its driver to read signals along the track, so a computer is used. It "reads ahead" and informs the driver of the proper speed and any necessary stops. Traveling at 165 miles per hour, the train would need about two _15_ to come to a full stop. For this reason, there are no places where vehicles may cross the tracks.

The French hope to extend service of their super-speed trains throughout France. They also hope to _16_ their trains to other countries.

---

10. a. oldest   c. fastest
     b. tallest   d. youngest

11. a. around   c. through
     b. between   d. above

12. a. years   c. volts
     b. tracks   d. dollars

13. a. easily   c. carefully
     b. slowly   d. fully

14. a. knife   c. shape
     b. window   d. track

15. a. dollars   c. hours
     b. tracks   d. miles

16. a. wish   c. sell
     b. increase   d. carry

In this photo, a young man is making a speech. What is the purpose of his speech? What opinions does he have, and how does he back them up? Anyone listening to his speech would have to decide.

When you read an article, the same kinds of questions are important. What is the purpose of the article? What opinions are given, and how are they supported? Thinking about such questions as you read is called *critical reading*.

Most reading tests include questions about the opinions in an article, and the reasons the article was written. The purpose of Part 3 is to help you learn how to answer those kinds of questions.

The following article is from a doctor's column in a magazine. Use the details in the article to decide why it was written. Think about the writer's opinions. Then answer the questions below the article.

Sports Smarts

These days, it seems, almost everyone is doing some kind of sport. I'm glad. Regular exercise can keep you lean and fit. But there's a bad side to any kind of fitness or sports activity — *injuries*.

You can keep from getting hurt by "listening" to your body. If you start to feel aches and pains, slow down or stop for a while. Pain is a warning. Many people suffer serious injuries in sports because they don't stop when they first feel pain.

If you pay attention, your body will usually give you warning of wear-and-tear injuries. Whatever your sport, if you feel pain and it gets worse as you continue, quit and go home!

Choose the best answer for each question.

1. Why is the author glad that people are taking part in sports?
   a. Sports are for everyone.
   b. Sports help to pass time.
   c. Sports can keep people healthy.
   d. Sports can cause injuries.

2. Why did the author write the article?
   a. to give rules for exercising
   b. to warn about sports injuries
   c. to ask everyone to choose a sport
   d. to suggest a treatment for pain

3. What is the author's opinion about small aches and pains?
   a. Exercise can prevent them.
   b. They always happen in sports.
   c. They should be treated by a doctor.
   d. They can lead to serious injuries.

Check your answers. You should have chosen **c** for 1, **b** for 2, and **d** for 3. If you missed Question 1, check the details in the first paragraph. If you missed Question 2, quickly review all the details in the article. For Question 3, look for the right detail near the phrase *aches and pains*.

Read the following selection and answer the questions.

Shopping for Bargains

Few people can resist a bargain. But bargains are not always what they seem. Some sales and bargains are good deals, but not all are. Here are some pointers to help you tell the difference between real bargains and bad deals.

Sometimes a product is on sale for "below manufacturer's cost." Watch out for this kind of "bargain." Why would anyone want to sell a product for less than it cost to make it? Before buying, you should find out why it is being sold at a loss to the manufacturer. Is it damaged? Is it out of style? Does it come with any guarantee?

Another pointer is to read price tags on sale items carefully. For example, a price tag in a store may say "regular price $16." The regular price is the price of the item before the sale started and after the sale ends. The regular price is only for that store, however. In another store, the price could be lower.

A price tag may also say "original price $16." That means at one time the item sold for $16 — even as much as five years earlier! For example, the original price of pocket calculators was high when they were introduced. Now the price is much lower. Showing the original price would be misleading.

Finally, be careful how you use cents-off coupons. A coupon can save you money only if you intend to use the item. The price of an item may vary at different stores, so use the coupon at the store with the lowest price. Don't forget to add any sales tax to the item before you figure out the "cents-off" price.

Choose the best answer for each question.

1. Why did the author write the article?
   a. to show that there are no real bargains
   b. to warn the reader that some sales are not bargains
   c. to sell a certain product
   d. to warn the reader not to spend money on bargains

Check your answer. If you can tell the main idea of the article, you will usually know the author's purpose in writing it. The same words are in several answer choices, so be sure to choose the right one. The answer is **b**.

2. Which of these statements is an opinion?
   a. Few people can resist a bargain.
   b. A tax adds to the price of an item.
   c. The regular price is the price before or after a sale.
   d. The price of pocket calculators has dropped.

Check your answer. Can you tell an opinion from a fact? Answer choices **b**, **c**, and **d** are facts. There is only one opinion — a statement that can be argued. An opinion is a belief that someone thinks is true. The right answer is **a**.

3. What is the author's opinion of an item that sells below manufacturer's cost?
   a. It is out of style.
   b. It is always a good deal.
   c. It has no guarantee.
   d. There may be something wrong with the item.

Check your answer. Look for the phrase *below manufacturer's cost* in the article and read the author's advice. The answer is **d**.

4. How does the author suggest that cents-off coupons should be used?
   a. only for items with no tax
   b. for as many items as possible
   c. in stores with the lowest prices
   d. only at the largest store

Check your answer. The last paragraph of the article has advice on using cents-off coupons. The facts you need are clearly stated in the paragraph. The answer is **c**.

Read the next passage. Use the details to answer all the questions. Then check your answers.

In Defense of Crows

To the Editor:

I was unhappy about the article in your newspaper called "Nothing To Crow About." Your article stated that crows are birds that do more harm than good. Nothing can be further from the truth. I have been watching a large flock of crows in my area. I have discovered that crows are clever birds that really do benefit farmers.

It is true that crows kill chickens and steal eggs. That makes crows unpopular with farmers. But chickens and eggs are part of a crow's diet. Crows must eat to stay alive, like any other creature. Crows are actually helpful to farmers. These birds eat worms, grasshoppers, and other harmful insects.

Crows are too clever to be fooled by scarecrows. Crows know that straw and bits of cloth can't harm them. And they prove it by perching on the outstretched arms of a scarecrow.

Your article blamed crows for attacking owls. I have seen crows dive-bomb owls many times. However, the owls are almost never injured. They seem to expect that crows will attack them. In any real fight between crows and owls, it is the crows that would be hurt. After all, the owls are the bigger birds.

Crows themselves are often attacked by smaller birds. I have seen many crows with missing wing feathers.

I will admit that crows steal things, such as coins and clothespins. They even steal watches and diamond rings. If it can be carried, a crow will steal it. Unfortunately, crows have no use for any of these things. To me, this simply shows that crows are curious.

Being curious is just one of the many good traits that crows have. I think that crows deserve more respect than they have been getting.

Choose the best answer for each question.

1. This passage is ___.
   a. a fable
   b. part of a diary
   c. a letter to a newspaper
   d. a newspaper article

2. Which of these statements is an opinion?
   a. Crows attack owls.
   b. Crows feed on chickens.
   c. Crows steal things.
   d. Crows are helpful birds.

3. What is the author's purpose in writing about crows?
   a. to show that crows make good pets
   b. to show that crows have some good traits
   c. to prove that crows are harmful
   d. to show that farmers and crows can work together

4. The author excuses the fact that crows steal by claiming that __.
   a. stealing is not important
   b. crows don't steal valuable objects
   c. crows are simply curious
   d. crows like to collect shiny objects

5. Which of these did the author rely on most in forming opinions about crows?
   a. personal observation   c. discussions with farmers
   b. reports from books   d. a course on birds

Check your answers.

Question 1: When you can identify what kind of passage you are reading, you are practicing critical reading. The heading *To the Editor* and the first sentence are the clues you need. The answer is **c.**

Question 2: Answer choices **a, b,** and **c** are facts about crows. They are stated as facts in the letter. People might disagree with answer choice **d,** an opinion. The answer is **d.**

Question 3: For what purpose was this letter written? You can discover the purpose by reviewing the writer's opinions about crows. The answer is **b.**

Question 4: Find the details about things that crows steal. The details are near the end of the passage. Use them to choose the best answer. The answer is **c.**

Question 5: Many details in the passage suggest that the author made a regular habit of crow-watching. The answer is **a.**

Read the next selections. Practice your critical-reading skills by using details to answer the questions.

The following is part of a journal.

Inside the Jungle

I have now spent a week in the Amazon jungle in Brazil. The jungle is filled with many kinds of animals, birds, and fish. But chances of seeing these creatures are slim, because they are easily frightened. Crocodiles, turtles, electric eels, and fish live in the Amazon River.

During a canoe ride one night, I sat quietly for almost an hour, trying to spot some of the jungle's creatures. With a flashlight, I finally saw squirrel monkeys running along tree branches. A crocodile eyed our canoe as it moved through the water. On our return to camp, I saw a large, hairy tarantula sitting on a tree stump.

Several native tribes make their homes along the banks of the Amazon River. For most of them, their style of living has hardly changed in the past 4,000 years. I visited a village of the Yagua tribe. The people were interested in me, but cautious. The Yagua are shy people who will probably never get used to the sight of tourists.

The Yagua live on high wooden platforms covered by thatched roofs. They eat whatever the jungle supplies, including fish, bananas, and yucca plants.

The men wear grass skirts and hats. They paint red dye made from berries on their faces and necks. The women and children wear skirts of cloth and shirts of straw, but are not "made up" as the men are. The

men spend the day hunting with blowguns that shoot poison darts. Meanwhile, the women and children keep the village in good order and make beads and the blowguns.

Before I left the village, the children asked me to write my name for them. They watched me with great interest as I wrote. I was sad to leave the village but grateful that the Yagua had been willing to share their lives with me.

Choose the best answer for each question.

1. The journal tells mainly of the author's ___.
   a. conversations with the Yagua tribe
   b. travels in the Amazon jungle
   c. canoe trip on the Amazon River
   d. life in a native village

2. The author probably wrote the journal to ___.
   a. persuade readers to travel to the jungle
   b. persuade people to live in simple ways
   c. share the experience of traveling in a faraway place
   d. show that life along the Amazon River is lonely

3. What reason does the author give for seeing few jungle creatures?
   a. The animals were easily frightened.
   b. Most of the animals slept during the night.
   c. Crocodiles scared the animals away.
   d. The Yagua kept the animals as pets.

4. Which of the following is an opinion?
   a. I visited a village of the Yagua tribe.
   b. The men spend the day hunting for food.
   c. They eat whatever the jungle supplies.
   d. The people were interested in me, but cautious.

5. Which is probably most important in watching for jungle creatures?
   a. excitement   c. strength
   b. patience   d. fear

6. What kinds of details about the Yagua did the author *not* include in the journal?
   a. their diet   c. their hunting weapons
   b. their clothing   d. their schools

Take a Walk

Many people run for sport or exercise. But what if you are not a "born" runner or jogger? You may still want a sport that's inexpensive and easy to do. Why not try walking?

Walking is something that almost any normal, healthy person can do. It requires no special equipment. Walking can give you many of the same benefits as jogging or running; it will just take longer. Jogging and running make your heart and lungs work harder than walking. They also put more stress on your legs and feet than walking does.

The problem with walking as a kind of exercise is that most people don't take it seriously. But there's a big difference between serious walking and the kind of walking that most of us do. Walking, like jogging, should have a steady and continuous motion.

If you're going to get your exercise by walking, you need to have your own walking program. After all, runners and joggers set goals for themselves. Walkers need goals, too.

Set a definite course to walk. Start by walking about 15–30 minutes a day. Build up your time and distance slowly. Try increasing your walking speed little by little.

If jogging or running is your sport, follow the same advice. Start off slowly. Spend most of the first few days just walking. Then start walking and running on the same day. Run or jog a short distance, then walk for a while, then run, then walk. Follow that pattern for 15–30 minutes a day. Slowly make each run longer and each walk shorter. Later on, you can increase your distance, speed, and exercise time.

Choose the best answer for each question.

1. Which of these statements supports the idea that walking is an inexpensive sport?
   a. It is a kind of exercise.
   b. It requires a regular program.
   c. It has many of the same benefits as running.
   d. It requires no special equipment.

2. According to the article, walking should be done ___.
   a. in stops and starts
   b. as fast as possible
   c. at a steady pace
   d. at the same time as jogging

3. In the author's opinion, how are running and walking alike?
   a. They require goals.
   b. They cause the same amount of stress.
   c. They have the same effect on the heart.
   d. They take the same amount of time.

4. Which of these would the author probably *not* consider serious walking?
   a. walking 15 minutes a day
   b. walking while window shopping
   c. increasing your speed little by little
   d. walking just before jogging

5. Which advice would the author probably agree with?
   a. Increase your walking distance by one-fourth mile each day.
   b. Jog 30 minutes a day to start.
   c. Increase your walking distance by two miles each day.
   d. Choose more active sports than walking.

6. The author probably believes that ___.
   a. everybody should walk or jog
   b. jogging is better exercise than walking
   c. some kind of exercise is desirable
   d. walking is better exercise than jogging

The Benefits of Puppy Love

"Have a talk with your dog and call me in the morning."
That's what doctors might say after reading the new studies about
people and their pets. The studies are showing that pets are good for
your health. It doesn't seem to matter whether your pet is a dog or a
lizard or a goldfish. Pets may do more for you than you will ever do for
them.

Suppose you have had a long and tiring day, and feel a little anxious.
The best way to unwind may be to chat with your cat or hug your
hamster.

A study of people and pets was done at the University of
Pennsylvania. This fact was discovered: The blood pressures of some
people who were studied stayed the same — or went down — when
they spoke to animals. Normal blood pressure is important to good
health. And, doctors say, blood pressure often goes up when people
talk to *people*!

Animals also seem to help people who are sick or lonely. People in
nursing homes showed great joy when pets were brought to them.
They liked to touch the animals and talk to them. And they liked to talk
to one another about the animals.

One man had suffered a stroke and had not spoken for a long time. A
puppy was placed on his wheelchair tray. Suddenly the man was
laughing softly. "Puppy," he whispered.

Patients at a mental hospital were given small animals, such as white
mice, birds, and guinea pigs. Caring for the pets gave these patients a
reason to talk and work together. Many became calmer and more
hopeful.

In France, a veterinarian found that pets helped children who would
not communicate with other people. The children first touched and
played with pets, then began speaking with adults.

Do animals have "magic" powers to help people? Scientists think the
magic is simply love and trust. Pets are likely to welcome people and
show them affection. They give people something to care about. They
make people feel wanted and needed.

The studies seem to show that animals are "good medicine." Maybe
the animals have known that all along.

Choose the best answer for each question.

1. The theory that pets are good for your health is ___.
   a. supported by experiments
   b. supported by the author's experience
   c. supported by opinions only
   d. not supported at all

2. After reading this article, you can conclude that ___.
   a. people with pets never get sick
   b. animals seem to produce good health
   c. pets should replace medicines
   d. everyone should have a pet

3. How could having pets in a nursing home cause problems?
   a. They need feeding and care.
   b. They may not be friendly to all the people there.
   c. Some people there may be afraid of pets.
   d. All of the above.

4. Why did silent or withdrawn children respond to pets?
   a. The pets were a change in treatment.
   b. The pets were beautiful animals.
   c. The children could play and talk with the pets.
   d. The pets made no noise.

5. Which of these is an opinion?
   a. Normal blood pressure is a sign of good health.
   b. A sick man responded to a puppy.
   c. Animals know when people are ill.
   d. Goldfish and lizards are kinds of pets.

LESSON 6

The following selection is an editorial. An editorial is an article stating the opinion of the newspaper or magazine.

Working for Nothing Pays Off

Volunteers have always played a big role in American life. In the early colonies, people were expected to use their spare time for their communities. Benjamin Franklin put that idea into practice when he set up a volunteer fire department for Philadelphia. Today, most rural communities and many small towns still depend on volunteers to fight fires.

The editors of this newspaper believe that volunteer work is as important as ever. A lot of people agree with us. One out of every four Americans does some kind of volunteer work. People take scout groups on camping trips. They spend weekends cleaning up town parks. They pick up litter along hiking trails. They visit the sick and the elderly. And those are only a few examples.

It is clear that volunteer work helps society. But what about the volunteers? What do they get out of their work, besides the good feeling of having helped others?

Most people usually can get valuable job experience and knowledge through volunteer work. Many volunteers can learn skills that help them to prepare for full-time jobs. Let's say you work as a volunteer in the office of a hospital or a public radio station. You type and file letters, and do fund raising on weekends and after school. And you do this for nothing. But when you look for paying jobs, the experience you gained as a volunteer may give you an edge over other job-seekers.

Of course, volunteer work may have nothing to do with the career you wish to follow. Does that mean there's no benefit in it for you? Not at all! Sometimes, volunteer work can teach you a lot about yourself — and that is probably the greatest benefit of all. It can help you decide which things you do best. It can help you learn about certain kinds of work. It can help you deal with people.

Service to the community is important. And your future is important, too. Isn't there something that you can volunteer to do right now? It's time to get started!

Choose the best answer for each question.

1. This editorial was written mainly to ___.
   a. describe volunteer work in colonial times
   b. describe volunteer work outdoors
   c. persuade readers to volunteer
   d. explain the difference between paid work and volunteer work

2. Why do small towns probably depend on volunteers?
   a. That has always been the custom.
   b. There is not enough money for paid workers.
   c. Enough people are willing to share their time.
   d. All of the above.

3. Which of these opinions would the editors agree with?
   a. Volunteering has some hidden benefits.
   b. People should always be paid for their work.
   c. Volunteers worked harder in colonial times than today.
   d. Volunteering must come before paid work.

4. One kind of volunteer work *not* mentioned in the article is ___.
   a. cleaning parks
   b. serving on first-aid squads
   c. fighting fires
   d. raising money for hospitals

5. How do the editors try to prove that volunteer work is important?
   a. by saying it is
   b. by showing many helpful volunteer activities
   c. by showing the need for volunteers
   d. by claiming that everyone does volunteer work

6. In the opinion of the editors, what is the greatest benefit of volunteer work?
   a. trying out new things
   b. preparing for a career
   c. working for a hospital
   d. exploring one's abilities and interests

Questions for the following selection are on pages 75–76.

How I Learned To High-Jump: Bill Cosby's Own Story

When I was in junior high school in Philadelphia, there was a fellow we called Sporty. One day after school, I saw him high-jumping alone in the gym. He had both high-jump stands up and three padded mats to break his fall. A bamboo pole stretched across the standards.

Sporty was jumping four feet, six inches. He began his approach with a certain number of steps. Then he planted his right foot and threw his left leg up. As he began to clear the bar, he flattened his body out and kicked his back leg up. He landed smoothly on his back. It looked simple. I wanted to do it.

But my jumping style was a lot different than Sporty's. My style was a sort of running-away-from-the-scene-of-the-crime jump. I ran, stopped, planted both legs, and jumped straight up. I brought my knees up to my chin, and crashed smack on the bamboo pole on the way down.

Sporty was very upset by my jump. After he had worked for weeks by himself, a fool came along and broke his pole.

Right around that time, Mr. Lister, our gym teacher, came by. Mr. Lister had jumped for Temple University, and I think his record was six feet, nine inches. To Sporty and me, that was out of this world. So, when he offered to teach us, we couldn't wait.

Mr. Lister decided that I needed work on my style. As I started my approach, I planted the left foot down and then stopped. I started up again with three fast steps. As I neared the bar, I jumped straight up, and brought both legs up in a sitting position. I came straight down on top of the bamboo pole and snapped it in half.

After I had broken three poles, I began to wonder if this sport was really for me. I thought I could be a jumper. I had proved that to myself in basketball by getting more rebounds than almost anyone else. I was one of the top gym-class athletes. So what was the problem?

Mr. Lister suggested that I start at the beginning. So I worked on my approach at the embarrassing height of two feet. I cleared the bar, but all I could do was grumble about it being so close to the ground.

The months passed and finally I was jumping four feet, six inches. Then Sporty moved the bar to four feet, nine inches. I made my approach and suddenly I was scared. This was too great a challenge. The bar was too high. I couldn't make the jump. The closer I got, the more convinced I became that I would miss it. So I did exactly what I thought I would do. I knocked the bar off.

When Sporty tried it, his back leg nicked the bar, but he made the jump. I figured that if Sporty could do it, I had better do it!

I took three steps, but that thought came back again: "It's too high. You won't make it." I didn't make it.

On his second jump, Sporty knocked the bar over. For some strange reason, I suddenly felt better. Now I could do it. I wasn't afraid of failing anymore.

I stood at the mark and blocked out all my negative thoughts. I approached the bar, planted my foot, and jumped. I sailed over the bar and my back leg hit. I knocked the bar off, but I had cleared it by a good six inches. My confidence returned. I put the bar up quickly, came back around, and made my approach again. I went up and over — six inches over. And this time the bar held.

When you believe in yourself, you can do anything.

Choose the best answer for each question.

1. The story the author tells is __.
   a. a fictional story
   b. the plot of a television series
   c. a true story about his own experiences
   d. a story about a sports hero

2. The author admired Mr. Lister because of the teacher's ___.
   a. friendliness
   b. high-jump record
   c. college experiences
   d. interest in sports

3. What lesson did Mr. Lister's instruction help the author to learn?
   a. Replace equipment that breaks.
   b. Practice once a week.
   c. Exercise before any sports contest.
   d. Start slowly and increase the effort.

4. In the third paragraph, how was the author's high-jump style like "running away from the scene of the crime"?
   a. His movements were jerky.
   b. He felt guilty when he jumped.
   c. He looked over his shoulder.
   d. He jumped with grace and skill.

5. How did the author react after breaking many high-jump poles?
   a. He gave up.
   b. He became jealous of Sporty's ability.
   c. He felt that he would never learn to high-jump.
   d. He was puzzled by all the trouble he was having.

6. What did the author do differently on his last jump?
   a. He speeded up his approach.
   b. He listened to the advice of his coach.
   c. He decided not to worry.
   d. He copied Sporty's style.

7. How did the author seem to feel about his successful high jump at the end of the story?
   a. He was proud of it.
   b. He wished he had jumped higher.
   c. He still wanted to beat Sporty's record.
   d. He was angry about failing the first time.

8. The author's purpose in writing this story was to ___.
   a. urge the reader to take part in sports
   b. warn that high jumping causes injuries
   c. teach the reader some high-jumping skills
   d. show the importance of self-confidence

Practice your critical-reading skills in the following two selections. Read the test tips before you read each selection. Put your answers on your answer sheet.

Test Tips: Some answer choices on tests are incorrect because they are not as complete as the correct choice. Choose the most complete answer.

If praise from music critics could guarantee record sales, Delbert McClinton would be a best-selling star. McClinton has had fine reviews from the critics. He has a devoted group of fans, but he deserves to be a superstar. Take this music critic's word for that.

McClinton is one of few singers with roots in both real blues and Southern rock. He began playing music as a teenager in Texas. Later, he and his band shared the stage with Jimmy Reed and Sonny Boy Williamson, the great blues players. They influenced McClinton's singing style and helped him learn to play blues harmonica.

McClinton began making records in the mid-1970's. His latest album is his most enjoyable so far. McClinton's lively singing and wailing harmonica breathe new life into old blues songs and give his new songs a real blues sound. When it comes to soulful, Southern-fried blues rock, McClinton's music is the real thing.

---

1. What is the writer's opinion of McClinton's success?
   a. He has never had any success.
   b. He is very successful.
   c. He has had some success but deserves more.
   d. He is not known outside of Texas.

2. With what other singer does the writer compare McClinton?
   a. Jimmy Reed
   b. Sonny Boy Williamson
   c. Paul Simon
   d. no other singer

3. The writer tries to persuade others that McClinton is good by saying that ___.
   a. he comes from Texas
   b. the critics praise him
   c. he played as a teenager
   d. he plays the harmonica

4. What is the writer's opinion of McClinton's latest album?
   a. It is better than his other albums.
   b. It is not well recorded.
   c. It is not as good as his other albums.
   d. It is the best album ever made.

Test Tips: When reading a poem, look for opinions and feelings that the poet is expressing. Questions on a test are likely to ask about a poet's opinions and feelings.

Spring Thunder

1 Listen. The wind is still,
2 And far away in the night —
3 See! The uplands fill
4 With a running light.

5 Open the doors. It is warm;
6 And where the sky was clear —
7 Look! The head of a storm
8 That marches here!

9 Come under the trembling hedge —
10 Fast, although you fumble.
11 There! Did you hear the edge
12 Of winter crumble?

Mark Van Doren

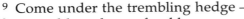

5. The poet reacts to a spring storm with a feeling of __.
   a. sadness   c. boredom
   b. excitement   d. anger

6. In *Line 4*, what is the "running light"?
   a. lightning
   b. a flashlight beam
   c. electric lights
   d. sunlight

7. The poet's description shows the storm is coming up __.
   a. slowly   c. suddenly
   b. quietly   d. carelessly

8. In *Lines 11 and 12*, what sound is described?
   a. the roar of the wind
   b. marching sounds
   c. the sound of drums
   d. the crash of thunder

9. How does the poet show that the storm is not something to fear?
   a. by standing on a hill
   b. by going outside to watch it
   c. by watching it from a window
   d. by waiting for clearing skies

UNIT II
VOCABULARY

PART 1: *Synonyms and Antonyms*   80

PART 2: *Context Clues*   110

PART 3: *Words with Several Meanings*   126

PART 4: *Word Parts*   138

PART 1 *Synonyms and Antonyms*

You often have to explain the meaning of a new word you come across in your reading or on a vocabulary test. In Part 1, you are going to practice two methods of understanding and explaining the meaning of an unfamiliar word. First, you will learn to define a new word by matching it with a word or phrase that has almost the same meaning. Next, you will learn to define a new word by matching it with a word or phrase that has the opposite meaning. Your matches will help you understand and correctly use the new words you will meet in Part 1.

Look for matches in the picture below. Try to find two signs that have almost the same meaning. Also, match two signs that have opposite meanings. Write your matches on your paper.

SYNONYMS AND MEANING

Sometimes two words have almost the same meaning. Words with almost the same meaning are called *synonyms*. The simplest way to explain the meaning of a word is to use its synonym as a definition.

For example, the words *falsehood* and *lie* are synonyms. One way to define a *falsehood* is to say that it means a "lie."

Most questions on vocabulary tests ask you to name the best synonym for a difficult word. Therefore, learning synonyms for new words can help you do better on vocabulary tests. Knowing synonyms can also help you understand materials that you read. Suppose you come across a hard word in your reading. If you can put a synonym in its place, you can understand the ideas in the reading more easily.

Read the paragraph below about some unusual facts in the life of one U.S. president. Three words in the paragraph are printed in dark type.

During President Benjamin Harrison's term in office (1889–1893), the **initial** use of electricity occurred in the White House. The idea of possessing electric lights **baffled** and frightened the Harrisons. They were afraid they would get a shock if they touched a light switch. As a **consequence**, lights in the White House often remained on round the clock. The Harrisons frequently slept in a brilliantly lit bedroom.

Which word in dark type is a synonym of *result*? Which word in dark type is a synonym of *first*? Which word in dark type is a synonym of *confused*?

Read the paragraph again. This time, substitute *first* for **initial**. Also, read *confused* in place of **baffled** and *result* in place of **consequence**. Did using the synonyms help you understand the paragraph more easily?

Do the activities on the next two pages. You will learn more about using synonyms to explain the meanings of new words.

A. Look at the words in List 1 below. They were all used in the paragraph about President Harrison. You will find a synonym for each word in List 2. Write the matches on your paper.

LIST 1
1. term
2. possessing
3. remained
4. frequently
5. brilliantly

LIST 2
a. brightly
b. owning
c. time
d. stayed
e. often

Check your answers. Reread the paragraph on page 81. Read the words in List 2 in place of their synonyms in List 1. Does the paragraph still make sense to you? If it does, then your answers are right.

B. Read the next paragraph about another U.S. president. Notice the words in dark type.

In 1893, President Grover Cleveland was **informed** that he had cancer. **Surgery** was done on Cleveland on a yacht. Most of his upper left jaw was removed. He **insisted** that the operation be kept secret. He was afraid that worries about his health might **aggravate** the difficult business problems the country was facing at the time. Cleveland was fitted with an **artificial** jaw made of hard rubber, and no one seemed to notice the difference. The secret was not revealed until 1917.

Now try to answer the following questions about the words in dark type in the paragraph you just read. Put your answers on your paper.

1. Which word is a synonym of *fake* or *man-made*?
2. Which word is a synonym of *demanded*?
3. Which word is a synonym of *operation*?
4. Which word is a synonym of *told*?
5. Which word is a synonym of *make worse*?

Check your answers. Reread the paragraph. Put the words from the questions in place of the words in dark type. Does the paragraph still make sense to you? If it does, then your answers are right.

C. Here are the kinds of questions you see often on vocabulary tests. Look at the word in dark type at the top of each item. Then pick the answer that means the same as the word in dark type. Put your answers on your paper.

1. baffled by the mystery
   a. confused
   b. demanded
   c. informed

2. her **initial** thought
   a. secret
   b. first
   c. surprising

3. shining **brilliantly**
   a. softly
   b. brightly
   c. darkly

4. possessing a new watch
   a. finding
   b. using
   c. owning

5. face the **consequences**
   a. results
   b. facts
   c. mirrors

6. aggravate a problem
   a. face
   b. solve
   c. make worse

Check your answers. You should have picked **a** for 1, **b** for 2, **b** for 3, **c** for 4, **a** for 5, and **c** for 6. If you didn't get those answers, read pages 81 and 82 again.

Here are the eight new words in this lesson. Next to each word is a word or phrase that has almost the same meaning. Look for the new words in the story below. Use the synonyms to help you understand the lesson words.

endorsed—approved
competitive—decided by a contest
maximum—highest possible point
obligation—duty

adhere—stick or follow
regulations—rules
interfere—get in the way
promoted—advanced

BMX Racing

BMX is the fastest growing kids' sport in the U.S. today. It involves bicycle racing on homemade tracks in the backyard. Recently, the National Bicycle League **endorsed** backyard racing as a **competitive** sport.

All you need to participate in BMX is a bicycle with wheels that are a **maximum** of 20 inches. But riders have an **obligation** to **adhere** to several safety measures.

Riders on BMX tracks must wear helmets and mouth protection. They must also wear long pants, long sleeve shirts and shoes, usually sneakers.

There are also safety **regulations** which apply to the bikes. The crossbars, handlebars and frame must be padded. The handlebars must have handgrips. Kickstands, chain guards, reflectors and other gadgets must be removed. This is to make sure that nothing will **interfere** with the motion of the wheels.

BMX races are called MOTOS. When you sign up for a race, you are given your MOTO number and the number of the gate where your MOTO begins. You run at least three MOTOS at each race. Your final score is based on your finishes in each of the three MOTOS. The NBL keeps track of points you earn at any track in the country. As you get older, you are **promoted** to a higher age class.

BMX racing is open to boys and girls. There is even a division called Cruiser Class. It is for people over 35. It was formed because so many parents enjoyed racing with their children, but weren't allowed to race against them. Now families can compete together in this thrilling new sport.

A. Decide which one of the lesson words should be used to fill the blank in each sentence below. Use the synonyms on page 84 to help you choose the right answers. Also notice the way the new words were used in the story. Write your answers on your paper.

1. A __ examination will decide who gets the job.
2. The coach posted a set of __ for the team to follow.
3. Unless you pass this class, you will not be __ to the next grade.
4. The principal __ a concert to raise money for the homeless.
5. The stadium holds a __ of four thousand people.
6. All those parties are going to __ with your schoolwork.
7. The new student tried to __ to the rules in his new school.
8. It is everyone's __ to help clean up after Saturday's dance.

B. Look at the word in dark type in each item below. Decide which answer is a synonym of the word in dark type. Put your answers on your paper.

1. **maximum** protection
   a. least
   b. most
   c. close

2. had an **obligation**
   a. interest
   b. opportunity
   c. duty

3. **endorsed** by the committee
   a. approved
   b. denied
   c. decided

4. **promoted** to general
   a. spoke
   b. returned
   c. advanced

C. Write a sentence to answer each question below. Use the lesson word in dark type in your answer.

1. Which school **regulation** annoys you the most?
2. What **competitive** sport would you like to play?
3. When did an adult ever **interfere** with your plans?

LESSON 2

Here are the eight new words in this lesson. Next to each word is a word or phrase that has almost the same meaning. Look for the new words in the story below. Use the synonyms to help you understand the lesson words.

proposed — suggested   **calculated** — measured
visualize — see or picture   **capacity** — volume or fullness
continuously — constantly   **emerged** — came out
quantity — amount   **massive** — huge

Making a Million

You may know how to write the number 1,000,000. But have you ever seen what a million of anything looks like? The students at River Dell Junior High School in New Jersey know just how big a million can be.

In May 1982, two math teachers at the school **proposed** an experiment. They suggested that students pop a million kernels of popcorn. In that way, the students would be able to **visualize** how large a million is.

Students brought in seven hot-air popcorn poppers from home. They also gathered more than 600 cups of popcorn. They had figured out that each cup held an average of 1,640 kernels of corn. The popcorn weighed 280 pounds.

The poppers were turned on and ran **continuously** during school hours. For five days, popcorn poured out of the machines. The students kept track of the **quantity** of kernels popped. They **calculated** the volume and weight of the growing pile of popcorn. The students also agreed not to eat any of the scientific material they created.

Toward the end of the experiment, every closet and office in the school was filled to its **capacity**. So students used a classroom to store the rest of their million.

Finally, on the fifth day, the one-millionth kernel of popcorn **emerged** from the poppers. The **massive** heaps of popcorn were gathered and dumped into a plastic container 16 feet long, 4 feet wide, and 2 feet deep. Several students took measurements and determined that the million kernels of popcorn would stretch 15.7 miles if they were laid end to end. That's how big a million kernels of popcorn is!

A. Decide which one of the lesson words should be used to fill the blank in each sentence below. Use the synonyms on page 86 to help you choose the right answers. Also notice the way the new words were used in the story. Write your answers on your paper.

1. The miners __ from the cave in which they had been working.
2. Irv carefully __ the distance between his house and the school.
3. Sandy's stomach was filled to its __ when she ate 10 hamburgers.
4. The mayor __ that the new school be built on River Road.
5. Pat talked __ on the telephone for more than two hours.
6. The store manager ordered a large __ of appliances to sell.
7. The architect drew a sketch to help us __ the shape of the new building.
8. In the junkyard were __ heaps of old car parts.

B. Look at the word in dark type in each item below. Decide which answer is a synonym of the word in dark type. Put your answers on your paper.

1. calculated the results
   a. listed
   b. saw
   c. measured

2. a **massive** traffic jam
   a. huge
   b. car
   c. frightening

3. emerged from a hole
   a. dug
   b. came out
   c. stayed away

4. visualize an idea
   a. picture
   b. object to
   c. remember

C. Write a sentence to answer each question below. Use the lesson word in dark type in your sentence.

1. If you walked **continuously**, how long would it take you to go 10 miles?
2. What is the largest **quantity** of people you have ever seen in one place?
3. How many people would it take to fill the school auditorium to **capacity**?

Here are the eight new words in this lesson. Next to each new word is a word or phrase that has almost the same meaning. Look for the new words in the story below. Use the synonyms to help you understand the lesson words.

torment — pain or suffering
decrease — reduce
dangled — hung
acute — sharp or strong

accustomed — used
throb — pound or beat
treatment — process or cure
consult — discuss

An Upside-Down Cure

Dr. Robert M. Martin has an unusual way to help patients reduce back **torment**. He tells them to hang upside down.

When people stand up, gravity puts pressure on their spines, Dr. Martin says. The result can be a painful backache. But by hanging upside down, people can **decrease** that pressure.

Martin has invented a special pair of ankle holders called Inversion Boots™ or Gravity Boots™. The ankle holders have a hook in front that can be attached to a bar. People take the ankle holders home or to a gym. They attach them to a chinning bar and hang from it. Martin estimates that nearly 300,000 people, including many professional athletes, use Gravity Boots.

Martin and his wife have **dangled** upside down a half hour a day for many years. Some people with **acute** back pains may hang even longer.

Martin says people don't get dizzy from hanging upside down. They might feel a little lightheaded at first, but they soon become **accustomed** to it. Also, blood doesn't **throb** in a person's head. In fact, Martin sometimes hangs upside down to get rid of a headache.

Martin's **treatment** may not be for everyone. He warns people with physical problems to **consult** with a doctor before trying Gravity Boots.

A. Decide which one of the lesson words should be used to fill the blank in each sentence below. Use the synonyms on page 88 to help you choose the right answers. Also notice the way the new words were used in the story. Write your answers on your paper.

1. After her knee injury, Angela suffered a great deal of __.
2. The patient complained that she had __ pains in her side.
3. The doctor suggested a __ of hot baths and aspirin.
4. Many people use cough drops to __ the pain of sore throats.
5. Sal's temple began to __ after he was hit in the head by a baseball.
6. Your muscles may hurt until you become __ to doing exercises.
7. You should always __ with a doctor before starting a new diet.
8. The man __ from a high ledge until the fire fighter rescued him.

B. Read each incomplete sentence below. Decide which answer best completes the sentence. Put your answers on your paper.

1. An **acute** pain is very __.
   a. mild
   b. sharp
   c. easy to heal

2. If you **consult** with someone, you __.
   a. fight
   b. walk
   c. discuss

3. If your heart is **throbbing**, it is __.
   a. not moving
   b. pounding
   c. broken

4. If a key chain **dangled** from someone's belt, it __.
   a. hung down
   b. fell down
   c. was lost

C. Write a sentence to answer each question below. Use the lesson word in dark type in your sentence.

1. What time are you **accustomed** to getting up every morning?
2. What do you do to **decrease** the pain of a headache?
3. What is another good **treatment** for curing backaches?

Here are the eight new words in this lesson. Next to each new word is a word or phrase that has almost the same meaning. Look for the new words in the story below. Use the synonyms to help you understand the lesson words.

currency — money
manufactured — made
duplicate — imitate or copy
federal — national

minted — coined or made
redeem — trade in or exchange
mutilated — torn
intact — whole or undamaged

Dollar Facts

You probably see or spend dollar bills every day. But how much do you know about the dollar? Here are some facts you may not know about the dollar bill and its history.

Every day, the U.S. government prints about $30 million in paper **currency**. The new bills replace older ones that have become worn out or torn. Most of the new bills are singles. A one-dollar bill lasts only about one-and-a-half years before it needs to be replaced. The smallest bill ever printed in the United States was a three-cent note printed in 1864. The largest was a $100,000 bill.

The paper used for U.S. currency is **manufactured** by the Crane Paper Company in Dalton, Massachusetts. The paper is strong enough so bills can be folded 4,000 times without tearing. The paper is made from a special formula. A special pattern of red and blue threads is woven into the paper. This makes the paper almost impossible to **duplicate**. It is a **federal** crime to make any paper that is similar.

Early in U.S. history, there were no dollar bills. Only dollar coins were **minted**. People had little faith in paper money at the time. Then, in 1862, Congress decided to print paper dollars.

Before 1889, you could **redeem** a sliced dollar bill for exact change. For example, if you had 30 percent of a dollar bill, a bank would give you 30 cents for it. Soon too many people were cutting apart their bills to get change, so the government decided to stop allowing these exchanges. Today, you may trade in a **mutilated** bill for its full value. But to get your money, more than half of the bill must be **intact**.

A. Decide which one of the lesson words should be used to fill the blank in each sentence below. Use the synonyms on page 90 to help you choose the right answers. Also notice the way the new words were used in the story. Write your answers on your paper.

1. A law that applies to everyone in a nation is a ___ law.
2. The country ___ a new coin to honor its first president.
3. The paper was ___ when it became caught in the machine.
4. The criminal tried to ___ the way the person signed his name.
5. Many people ___ trading stamps for gifts.
6. The car was ___ by a company in Detroit.
7. Even though it fell on the floor, the glass remained ___.
8. Many people don't like to carry much ___ in their wallets.

B. Read each incomplete sentence below. Decide which answer best completes the sentence. Put your answers on your paper.

1. When something becomes **mutilated**, it is ___.
  a. torn
  b. unhappy
  c. valuable

2. When you **duplicate** something, you ___.
  a. tear it
  b. copy it
  c. return it

3. If something is **intact**, it is ___.
  a. broken
  b. injured
  c. whole

4. The country **minted** new ___.
  a. paper money
  b. laws
  c. coins

C. Write a sentence to answer each question below. Use the lesson word in dark type in your answer.

1. What is the largest piece of **currency** you have ever seen?
2. Why is special paper **manufactured** for U.S. money?
3. Are **federal** laws passed by the U.S. Congress or by state legislatures?

Here are the 10 new words in this lesson. Next to each new word is a word or phrase that has almost the same meaning. Look for the new words in the story below. Use the synonyms to help you understand the lesson words.

employment — work
founded — formed or created
canceled — called off
disturbed — bothered
recreation — amusement or fun

attire — clothing
attracted — lured or appealed to
hospitality — kindness
thrive — grow or succeed
economic — financial or money

A New Baseball League

During World War II, millions of American men left their jobs and joined the armed forces. At the same time, millions of women replaced the men in factories and offices. Women athletes also found a new area of **employment** at that time — professional baseball. In 1943, the All American Girls Baseball League (AAGBL) was **founded**.

The major league baseball season was almost **canceled** in 1943. Nearly half of the professional baseball players had joined the armed forces. Some people feared there would not be enough players to keep the leagues going. This idea **disturbed** many people, including President Roosevelt. He felt that American factory workers needed some form of **recreation**. Watching baseball allowed them to take their minds off work and the war for a little while.

One baseball team owner decided to form a new professional league of women players. There were already thousands of women's softball teams playing in the United States and Canada. Major league scouts were sent to watch these teams. The best players were invited to try out for the new league. The players received $40 to $85 a week. That was good pay in the early 1940's.

Teams in the AAGBL played a game that was a mixture of baseball and softball. In addition, the women had to follow some special rules. They wore "feminine" **attire** — short dresses and knee socks. They were not to smoke or drink. Their dates had to be approved by their team's female chaperone.

The AAGBL quickly **attracted** many fans. The league started with four teams. By 1948, it had expanded to 10 teams. Almost a million fans attended games each year.

In league cities, people showed a special **hospitality** toward the players. Players from out of town stayed at fans' houses. Players who hit home runs or pitched shutouts often received gifts.

The women's league continued to **thrive** even after the war ended. Soon men's teams became interested in some of the better players. In 1950, a men's minor league team wanted to hire a woman to play first base. But the head of the AAGBL refused to sell the woman's contract. He felt her team needed her more. Another baseball manager is said to have wanted to hire a top woman shortstop. He would have paid her $50,000, he said, "if she were a he."

By 1954, things in the U.S. began to change. Major league games were now being shown on TV. Many former AAGBL fans stayed home to watch these games. Also, many fans in the AAGBL teams' cities were facing hard **economic** times. They couldn't afford to go to the women's games. So, the league ended after 11 years.

Many people today, however, still remember the excitement and fun provided by the women's league games.

A. Decide which one of the lesson words should be used to fill the blank in each sentence below. Use the synonyms on page 92 to help you choose the right answers. Also notice the way the new words were used in the story. Write your answers on your paper.

1. The game was __ because the field was too wet to play on.
2. I like to visit Lenore because she shows such __ to her guests.
3. Many people like such forms of __ as bowling and soccer.
4. More and more people came to games, and the league began to __.
5. The proper __ for basketball is shorts, T-shirt, and sneakers.
6. The businesswoman __ a new company to manufacture aluminum bats.
7. The new company provided __ for many additional workers.
8. In difficult __ times, many people have to borrow money.
9. The exciting player __ many new fans to the ball park.
10. The visiting player was __ when the home-team fans booed him.

B. Look at each sentence below. Decide which answer is the best synonym for the word in italics in the sentence. Put your answers on your paper.

1. Sara likes playing chess for *amusement*.
   a. recreation
   b. employment
   c. hospitality

2. Fish are sometimes *lured* by artificial "flies."
   a. founded
   b. disturbed
   c. attracted

3. Introducing a new product helped the business *succeed*.
   a. attract
   b. thrive
   c. cancel

4. Edith's *kindness* helped her visitors feel welcome.
   a. employment
   b. attire
   c. hospitality

C. Write a sentence to answer each question below. Use the lesson word in dark type in your sentence.

1. What special **attire** do football players wear?
2. Have you ever **canceled** a date? Why?
3. In what job do you hope to find **employment** in the future?
4. Which was **founded** earlier, the U.S. Navy or the U.S. Air Force?
5. What is one **economic** problem that many people in the country face?

94

WORD REVIEW

Here are 10 facts you have learned in Lessons 1–5 of Part 1. The words in italics in the fact sentences are synonyms for the 10 lesson words listed below. Rewrite the sentences, using the lesson words to replace their synonyms.

1. One *duty* that teachers had in the 1880's was cleaning the school chimney.

2. If teachers in the 1880's would *stick* closely to the rules for five years, they would receive a raise of 75 cents a week.

3. Students at River Dell Junior High School in New Jersey popped 1,000,000 kernels of popcorn so they could *picture* how big a million is.

4. The students *measured* the size and weight of the popcorn and figured that the kernels would make a line 15.7 miles long.

5. People suffering from back *pain* can get relief by hanging upside down from a bar.

6. Hanging upside down can *reduce* the pressure that gravity puts on a person's spine.

7. It is against the law to *imitate* the special paper used for printing dollar bills.

8. *Torn* dollar bills can be redeemed for their full value as long as more than half of the bill is in one piece.

9. During World War II, a women's professional baseball league was *created*.

10. The league continued to *grow* even after the war ended and male baseball players returned to the country.

LESSON WORDS

duplicate	torment
obligation	founded
visualize	decrease
mutilated	adhere
thrive	calculated

ANTONYMS AND MEANING

Some words mean just the opposite of each other. Two words that have opposite meanings are called *antonyms*. You can often use an antonym to help you understand and define an unfamiliar word. You can say that the new word means just the opposite of its antonym. For example, the words *taut* and *loose* are antonyms. You know what *loose* means, and you know that *taut* has the opposite meaning. So you can figure out that *taut* must mean "tight" or "tense."

Sometimes you can change a word into its opposite by adding a prefix to the beginning of the word. Adding the prefix *un, in,* or *im* to the beginning of a word often changes the word into its antonym. For example, *uncertain* means "not certain," *incorrect* means "not correct," and *imperfect* means "not perfect." What do you think are the meanings of *unknown, indirect,* and *impossible*? Look for these prefixes. They can provide a helpful clue to the meaning of a new word.

Three words are printed in dark type in the following story about a U.S. president. Use antonyms to help you explain their meanings.

Many people today think it was **improper** for Chester A. Arthur to become president in 1881. According to law, all presidents must have been born in the United States. Two towns in Vermont **assert** that they are Arthur's birthplace. However, modern research seems to show that Arthur was actually born in Canada. If this claim is true, it was **unlawful** for him to become president.

Here are the three new words and their antonyms. Use the antonyms to help you define the words. Write the meanings on your paper.

improper — proper or correct
assert — deny
unlawful — lawful or legal

A. Read the following story about unusual facts in the life of another U.S. president. Notice the words in dark type.

In 1919, President Woodrow Wilson suffered a **severe** stroke. Doctors felt he would recover, but he might die if he had to make high-pressure decisions. They also felt it would be **unwise** for Wilson to resign. He might lose his will to live in that case. Wilson had always discussed his **significant** decisions with Edith, his wife. Now, Edith took over the decision-making herself since her husband was **incapable** of doing so. For the next two years, she ran the country as its **unofficial** president. Edith Wilson can be considered the first woman president.

Decide which word in dark type in the story is the best one to complete each sentence below. Put your answers on your paper.

1. *Official* or *proper* is the opposite of __.
2. *Mild* is the opposite of __.
3. *Able* is the opposite of __.
4. *Unimportant* is the opposite of __.
5. *Smart* is the opposite of __.

Check your answers. Clues in the reading should help you figure out that the right answers are: 1. unofficial, 2. severe, 3. incapable, 4. significant, and 5. unwise.

B. Read each vocabulary test item below. Choose the answer that means the opposite of the word in dark type. Make sure you choose an antonym. Don't pick a synonym. Put your answers on your paper.

1. assert an idea
  a. claim
  b. think
  c. deny

2. significant details
  a. important
  b. unimportant
  c. hidden

3. an **unlawful** act
  a. legal
  b. illegal
  c. brave

4. incapable of acting
  a. unable
  b. slow
  c. able

Check your answers. You should have picked **c** for 1, **b** for 2, **a** for 3, and **c** for 4.

Here are the eight new words in this lesson. Next to each new word is a word or phrase that has almost the same meaning. Look for the new words in the story below. Use the synonyms to help you understand the lesson words.

unlawfully — illegally
dispute — argument
violated — disobeyed
injustice — unfairness

oppose — go against
forfeit — give up or lose
improper — incorrect
settlement — agreement

Native Americans on the "Lawpath"

In 1969, Native Americans in Maine went on the "lawpath." They went to court to win back millions of acres of land. They said the land had been taken away from them **unlawfully** by the U.S. government in the 1800's.

The court **dispute** lasted 11 years, but the Indian tribes finally won. They were awarded $81.5 million as payment for their land.

Now other Indian tribes across the United States have gone to court to win back land taken from them many years ago. Some Indian claims involve only a few hundred acres. But in other cases, millions of acres of land are at stake.

Lawyers for the Native Americans have studied hundreds of old laws and treaties. They have discovered that white men often **violated** these laws and treaties in order to take land from the Indian tribes living on it. Everyone has agreed that the Indians had been done an **injustice**. But no one is sure how to right the wrongs.

Many Indian leaders say that money is not the issue. They want their land back so their people can return to their old ways of life. Recently, Sioux Indians in South Dakota were awarded $122.5 million for land taken from them. But many of the Indians **oppose** taking the money. By accepting the money, they feel they would **forfeit** their claim to the land.

The Indians' requests have caused many problems. The people living on the land now don't want to give it up. They bought their land and the houses on it long after the land was taken from the Indians. They feel it would be **improper** to take the land from them now.

The **settlement** in Maine may offer the best answer to the problem. Most of the $81.5 million the Native Americans were awarded will be used to buy land from the people now living on it. The rest of the money will be used to help tribe members find jobs and improve their living conditions.

A. Each word or phrase below means the opposite of one of the new words in this lesson. On your paper, write the lesson word that is an antonym for each one. Use the synonyms on page 98 to help you choose the right answers. Also notice the way the new words were used in the story.

1. argument
2. favor or support
3. correct or right
4. agreement

5. obeyed
6. legally
7. fairness or justice
8. gain

B. Choose a word or phrase that means the opposite of the word in dark type in each item below. Make sure you pick an antonym. Put your answers on your paper.

1. reached a **settlement**
   a. agreement
   b. argument
   c. place

2. an **improper** action
   a. right
   b. wrong
   c. thoughtless

3. **oppose** a law
   a. make up
   b. favor
   c. go against

4. settle a **dispute**
   a. town
   b. position
   c. agreement

C. Write a sentence to answer each question below. Use the lesson word in dark type in your sentence.

1. What often happens to people who have **violated** driving laws?
2. What person in the news recently has acted **unlawfully**?
3. Why would some Native Americans choose to **forfeit** their money awards?

Here are the eight new words in this lesson. Next to each new word is a word or phrase that has almost the same meaning. Look for the new words in the story below. Use the synonyms to help you understand the lesson words.

efficient — capable or skillful
exceptional — extraordinary
gracious — charming
unruffled — calm
tireless — untiring or energetic

unlimited — vast or endless
reluctantly — unwillingly or unhappily
appreciation — gratitude

The Perfect Secretary

Thomas van Beek, a Dutch businessman, was starting out in business. He needed an **efficient** secretary to help him. Van Beek interviewed many people, but none seemed good enough for the job.

Finally, van Beek interviewed Miss Neef. Her typing and shorthand skills were **exceptional**. Besides her fine office skills, Miss Neef had a **gracious** personality. Van Beek decided to hire her.

After only one week, van Beek was convinced he had made the right choice. Miss Neef ran the office smoothly. She handled all calls politely. She managed to stay **unruffled**, even when an emergency came up. Miss Neef was also **tireless**. Even when her boss ran out of energy, Miss Neef displayed an **unlimited** amount of pep.

For 12 years, Miss Neef continued to do her job excellently. She seemed to be able to do the work of two people. Then, Miss Neef

announced that she planned to retire. Van Beek **reluctantly** accepted her decision.

Van Beek organized a good-bye party to show his **appreciation** to Miss Neef. At the party, the boss learned the secret of how his faithful secretary had managed to have so much energy.

Two Miss Neefs showed up at the party. They were identical twins. The sisters had shared the job as van Beek's secretary. Each worked half-time and split the paycheck. For 12 years, van Beek never suspected that he had really hired two secretaries instead of one.

A. Each word or phrase below means the opposite of one of the new words in this lesson. On your paper, write the lesson word that is an antonym for each one. Use the synonyms on page 100 to help you choose the right answers. Also notice the way the new words were used in the story.

1. weary or exhausted
2. ordinary or average
3. rude
4. ingratitude or ungratefulness
5. willingly
6. incapable or unable
7. nervous
8. small or limited

B. Read each incomplete sentence below. Decide which answer best completes the sentence. Put your answers on your paper.

1. A **gracious** person is not __.
   a. charming
   b. tiny
   c. rude

2. An **unruffled** person is not __.
   a. nervous
   b. calm
   c. messy

3. An **unlimited** amount of money is not __.
   a. vast
   b. small
   c. expensive

4. An **exceptional** worker is not __.
   a. excellent
   b. energetic
   c. ordinary

C. Write a sentence to answer each question below. Use the lesson word in dark type in your sentence.

1. Which teacher in your school seems the most **tireless**?
2. How do you show your **appreciation** when people give you presents?
3. Why is it important to hire **efficient** workers?

Here are the 10 new words in this lesson. Next to each new word is a word or phrase that has almost the same meaning. Look for the new words in the story below. Use the synonyms to help you understand the lesson words.

dubious — doubtful
flourishing — growing or thriving
adversity — bad luck or misfortune
appealing — tempting
inexperienced — untrained or new

criticism — complaints
impolite — rude or not polite
formidable — difficult
diligence — hard work
courteously — politely

A Young Business Leader

When Gregg Navarez graduated from high school in Los Angeles, he borrowed $125 from a friend. He planned to use the money to start his own cleaning business. Some people were **dubious** that Gregg would ever be able to repay the loan. They were wrong. Within only three years, Gregg's business was **flourishing**. By the time he was 21, he was making up to $6,000 a month.

Gregg's success story was a result of hard work and good business sense. He also had to overcome a lot of **adversity** in order to succeed.

The idea of running a cleaning business was **appealing** to Gregg. He had heard that some cleaning services earned up to $30 an hour. So, together with a friend, he formed the West Coast Office Cleaning Service. Gregg used the $125 loan to have business cards printed. He also placed ads for his service in local newspapers.

At first, Gregg and his friend charged only $10 an hour. They were **inexperienced** and needed the customers. They borrowed a vacuum cleaner and other supplies from Gregg's home.

The two young men worked hard. But sometimes, customers would get angry if the partners scratched furniture or forgot to lock an office after they had finished. Gregg's partner hated the **criticism** and soon quit. But Gregg stayed on. He never became **impolite** to customers who complained. He always apologized and promised to do better the next time. Customers liked his good manners.

After several months, the business was growing. Gregg, however, began to feel ill. In the hospital, Gregg discovered he had diabetes. He spent four months learning to deal with the disease. By that time, Gregg had lost all of his customers to other cleaning services.

Gregg was set on beginning again. He knew the problems would be even more **formidable** this time. He had huge doctor and hospital bills to pay. He also had just bought a truck.

Slowly, Gregg built up the business again. His **diligence** paid off. In time, he became too busy to do every job he was offered. So he gave work to other cleaning services. Gregg got paid for finding them the work.

What are some of the secrets of Gregg's success as a business person? First, he says, you have to be willing to sell yourself and your services. You can't be too shy. Also, you should not be afraid to face problems. Be willing to ask questions to learn how to solve the problems and do a better job. Finally, you should always treat customers **courteously**. Getting angry only loses business.

A. Each word or phrase below means the opposite of one of the new words in this lesson. On your paper, write the lesson word that is an antonym for each one. Use the synonyms on page 102 to help you choose the right answers. Also notice the way the new words were used in the story.

1. certain
2. laziness
3. not tempting
4. rudely
5. good luck
6. expert or experienced
7. easy
8. withering or shrinking
9. courteous or well-mannered
10. praise

B. Look at each sentence below. Decide which answer is the opposite of the word in dark type in the sentence. Put your answers on your paper.

1. Anne Marie's business was **flourishing** because of the advertisements she used.
   a. growing
   b. withering
   c. building

2. Rocky was a **formidable** opponent for the champion to defeat.
   a. easy
   b. tall
   c. lazy

3. The worker received a raise because of her **diligence**.
   a. hard work
   b. poverty
   c. laziness

4. I often get **criticism** from my teacher because of my sloppy handwriting.
   a. help
   b. praise
   c. complaints

5. **Impolite** business people often insult their customers.
   a. rude
   b. courteous
   c. clever

6. Playing video games is **appealing** to many adults.
   a. not tempting
   b. enjoyable
   c. difficult

C. Write a sentence to answer each question below. Use the lesson word in dark type in your sentence.

1. What is one example of **adversity** that Gregg Navarez had to overcome?
2. Why would **inexperienced** workers get paid less than experts?
3. What is one way to treat a customer **courteously**?

Here are 10 facts you have learned in Lessons 6–8 of Part 1. Ten lesson words are in dark type in the fact sentences. Write the 10 lesson words on your paper. Next to each one, write one synonym and one antonym from the lists below.

1. Native Americans throughout the United States have begun court **disputes** to win back land taken from them in the past.

2. Tribes have been awarded millions of dollars because the white men **violated** old laws and treaties.

3. Many Indians **oppose** taking the money; they want the land instead.

4. Thomas van Beek, a Dutch businessman, hired a new secretary because she had **exceptional** office skills.

5. The new secretary did her job well and remained **unruffled**, even during emergencies.

6. Van Beek gave Miss Neef a good-bye party to show his **appreciation** for her excellent work.

7. He discovered that his secretary was **tireless** because she was really two people — identical twins.

8. When Gregg Navarez started his cleaning business, he was **inexperienced** at doing cleaning work.

9. Soon his business was **flourishing**, and he was able to pay off his debts.

10. One secret to Gregg's success is that he treats his customers **courteously** and never argues with them.

SYNONYMS		ANTONYMS	
growing	untrained	ingratitude	expert
arguments	go against	favor	withering
extraordinary	calm	agreements	nervous
energetic	disobeyed	obeyed	ordinary
politely	thankfulness	exhausted	rudely

For the items below, choose the word or phrase that means the same, or almost the same, as each word in dark type. Put your answers on your answer sheet. The test words come from Lessons 1–3.

Test Tips: Carefully read the phrase that contains the word in dark type. Decide if you have ever heard the phrase before. Then read all four answers. Use your past knowledge to help you pick the best synonym.

1. ran **continuously**
   a. constantly
   b. slowly
   c. awkwardly
   d. quickly

2. felt **acute** pain
   a. mild
   b. less
   c. sharp
   d. very little

3. listened to **lectures**
   a. doctors
   b. songs
   c. friends
   d. speeches

4. list of **regulations**
   a. names
   b. rules
   c. answers
   d. words

5. **dangled** from a ledge
   a. watched
   b. reached
   c. stood
   d. hung

6. **consult** with a doctor
   a. discuss
   b. become
   c. need
   d. agree

7. **proposed** an idea
   a. suggested
   b. discussed
   c. rejected
   d. asked for

8. filled to **capacity**
   a. emptiness
   b. fullness
   c. overflowing
   d. start

9. **quantity** of supplies
   a. order
   b. need
   c. excellence
   d. amount

10. **accustomed** to pain
   a. treated
   b. relieved
   c. used
   d. remembered

For the items below, choose the word or phrase that best completes each sentence. The key words in the sentences come from Lessons 4 and 5.

Test Tips: Read the incomplete sentence carefully. Decide which word you are being asked to define in the sentence. This is the key word. Look for the answer choice that is a synonym of the key word.

11. If you collect currency, you own __.
    a. stamps
    b. books
    c. autographs
    d. money

12. Your field of employment is your __.
    a. interest
    b. work
    c. products
    d. hobby

13. When people do things for recreation, they are having __.
    a. fun
    b. problems
    c. sickness
    d. food

14. If a toy is intact, it is __.
    a. broken
    b. expensive
    c. fun
    d. whole

15. In the U.S., federal law applies to all people in __.
    a. a school
    b. the nation
    c. a state
    d. a city

16. Another word for economic is __.
    a. real
    b. difficult
    c. financial
    d. rich

17. If people show you hospitality, they show __.
    a. kindness
    b. medical care
    c. money
    d. records

18. When you redeem a coupon, you __.
    a. keep it
    b. find it
    c. lose it
    d. trade it in

19. If a game is canceled, it is __.
    a. called off
    b. started
    c. tied
    d. fun

20. If you have some new attire, you have bought __.
    a. tools
    b. games
    c. clothes
    d. books

For the items below, choose the word or phrase that is most nearly the opposite of each word in dark type. Put your answers on your answer sheet. The test words come from Lessons 6–8.

Test Tips: Think about the meaning of the phrase. Then read all four answers carefully. Make sure you pick an antonym of the word in dark type.

---

21. did something **improper**
a. incorrect
b. correct
c. annoying
d. slowly

22. overcame **adversity**
a. enemies
b. friends
c. problems
d. good luck

23. a **gracious** personality
a. rude
b. kind
c. calm
d. charming

24. agreed to a **settlement**
a. treaty
b. deal
c. argument
d. time

25. **unlimited** money
a. limited
b. endless
c. too much
d. counterfeit

26. a **formidable** problem
a. difficult
b. easy
c. financial
d. good luck

27. an **appealing** idea
a. not tempting
b. exciting
c. strange
d. difficult

28. demonstrate **diligence**
a. kindness
b. rudeness
c. experience
d. laziness

29. do something **reluctantly**
a. unwillingly
b. politely
c. impolitely
d. willingly

30. fight **injustice**
a. battles
b. unfairness
c. fairness
d. improperly

For the items below, choose the answer that best completes each sentence. The test words come from Lessons 1–8.

Test Tips: Read all four answers carefully. Make sure you pick an antonym of the key word. Don't be tricked by a synonym or by a word that looks like a test word.

31. Emerged is the opposite of __.
    a. came out
    b. entered
    c. joined
    d. emergency

32. Efficient is the opposite of __.
    a. gracious
    b. incapable
    c. effortless
    d. helpless

33. Unruffled is the opposite of __.
    a. messy
    b. calm
    c. nervous
    d. rude

34. Decrease is the opposite of __.
    a. increase
    b. neat
    c. reduce
    d. allow

35. Exceptional is the opposite of __.
    a. exact
    b. extraordinary
    c. ordinary
    d. lazy

36. Massive is the opposite of __.
    a. large
    b. small
    c. broken
    d. kind

37. Unlawfully is the opposite of __.
    a. legally
    b. illegally
    c. politely
    d. quickly

38. Criticism is the opposite of __.
    a. crying
    b. complaints
    c. happiness
    d. praise

39. Tireless is the opposite of __.
    a. exhausted
    b. endless
    c. unlimited
    d. sleepless

40. Dubious is the opposite of __.
    a. doubtful
    b. serious
    c. difficult
    d. certain

In Part 2, you will learn a way to make a logical guess about the meaning of a new word you meet in your reading. You will learn to look for meaning clues within the sentences and paragraphs that you read. Notice how a new word is used. Then relate the word to other words and ideas in the reading. This will help you guess the word's meaning.

Look at the picture below. The picture illustrates the meaning of the word **scrutinize**. Look for clues in the picture to help you guess the meaning of **scrutinize**. Write your guess on your paper.

Suppose you come across an unfamiliar word in your reading. You can make a good guess about the word's meaning, even without looking in a dictionary. You can look for meaning clues in the words and sentences that come before and after the new word. The meaning clues that you can locate near a new word to help you define it are called *context clues*.

Practice using context clues to help you figure out the meaning of the word printed in dark type in the following story. Write your guess on your paper.

Jean Laffite was a French pirate who lived near New Orleans in the early 1800's. Laffite escaped from U.S. authorities and took more than $10 million in stolen treasure with him. Some say his boat went aground on a sandbar near Corpus Christi, Texas. There, he buried his **loot**. People have been searching for the stolen property for many years. But no one has ever found it.

Check your answer. Think about what happened. You know that Laffite had stolen property with him and buried it. The words *stolen property* are even used in the sentence after the one with the new word in it. All these clues help you know that **loot** means "stolen property."

You should look for different kinds of context clues when you read to help you define new words that you meet. You will learn to use five different kinds of clues in the following activities.

CLUE 1: DEFINITION CLUE

Sometimes you will find the meaning of a new word given right before or after the word. The definition will be in the same sentence. Look for a definition clue below to help you know what **demise** means.

The British pirate Edward Teach, known as "Blackbeard," is supposed to have buried treasure in hundreds of places. One likely place is Ocracoke Island, off the coast of North Carolina. In 1718, Blackbeard met his **demise**, or death, near Ocracoke. Some people think the largest part of his treasure is hidden on the island.

Check your answer. The words *or death* come right after **demise**. They tell you that **demise** means "death."

CLUE 2: SERIES CLUE

Sometimes a new word will be part of a group of words that go together. You can figure out the meaning of the new word by studying the other words in the series. Use a series clue to help you know what **cruelty** means in the story below.

Captain William Kidd was hanged in 1701 for piracy, murder, and **cruelty** toward members of his crew. Before his death, he gave his wife a piece of parchment on which was written 44-10-66-18. The numbers seemed to be the map location of Deer Isle, Maine. People searched the island, but did not find any treasure there.

Check your answer. Cruelty is in a series with other crimes and harsh actions. You can guess that **cruelty** means "harshness" or "meanness."

CLUE 3: SYNONYM CLUE

Sometimes you can spot a synonym of an unfamiliar word in a sentence near the one in which the new word appears. Look for a synonym of **concealed** in the next buried-treasure story to help you define the word.

Some people think Jean Laffite also **concealed** treasure on Padre Island off the Texas coast. John Singer searched the island for the treasure Laffite hid there. He found a chest containing $80,000 worth of gold and jewels. He reburied it for safekeeping during the Civil War. He was unable to find it again after the war.

Check your answer. In the story, the word *hid* is used in the sentence after the one in which **concealed** appears. You can tell from the way the words are used that **concealed** and *hid* are synonyms.

CLUE 4: ANTONYM CLUE

Sometimes you can spot an antonym of a new word in a sentence near the one in which the new word appears. The antonym can help you define the unfamiliar word. Look for an antonym in the following story to help you guess what **unearthed** means.

In April 1934, FBI agents surrounded John Dillinger and his criminal gang near Mercer, Wisconsin. Dillinger escaped. Supposedly, he dug a hole behind his hideout and buried a suitcase containing nearly $200,000 there. Dillinger was soon killed by the FBI. The suitcase was never **unearthed**, however.

Check your answer. You can tell from the story that **unearthed** and *buried* are opposites. So you can guess that **unearthed** means "dug up."

CLUE 5: EXPERIENCE CLUE

Sometimes you can guess the meaning of an unfamiliar word because the meaning makes sense to you. The meaning fits with things you know to be true about a subject. Use your experience to guess the meaning of **sacred** in the following story.

In 1848, three Mexican brothers discovered a gold mine said to be worth $100 million in the Superstition Mountains in Arizona. The mine was located in a mountain that was important to the religion of the Apache Indians. The Apaches were angry that their **sacred** mountain was being harmed. They attacked and killed most of the mining party and hid the veins of gold with dirt. Many other prospectors have searched for the mine unsuccessfully.

Check your answer. You know that something important to a religion is holy. Therefore, you can guess that **sacred** means "holy."

Here are the eight new words in this lesson. Their meanings are not listed. Look for the new words in the story below. Try to find context clues to help you define the lesson words. You will find some hints to help you in the questions on the next page.

fad	eliminated
marathon	penalty
zany	jostled
spectators	frayed

Marathon Dancing

During the 1920's and the early 1930's, a new **fad** swept across the United States. This popular hobby was the dance **marathon**. It was a long contest to see which couple danced longest without stopping.

The record was set in Pittsburgh in 1932. A couple there danced for 24 weeks and 5 days straight. That's almost half a year!

Why did people take part in dance marathons? Some did it just to be **zany**. But most were more serious. They entered the contests because they were broke and needed the prize money — around $500 for a winning couple.

Marathons were often held in large sports arenas. **Spectators** paid 25 or 50 cents to watch the dancers. They cheered for their favorite couples. Sometimes they threw coins on the dance floor.

According to the rules, dancers had to stay on their feet and keep moving at all times. If their knees touched the floor, they were **eliminated** from the contest. If they stopped moving, the judge would give them a **penalty**. The punishment might be a sharp rap on the legs.

After each hour of dancing, a loud bell rang. That signaled a 15-minute rest period. Some dancers lay on cots, and others took showers. Nurses checked the dancers' hearts, and trainers rubbed swollen feet.

The couples grew weaker every day. Dancers slapped, kicked, or **jostled** their partners to keep them awake. Often one partner slept while being held up by the other.

After several days, nerves became **frayed**, or strained. Fights often broke out in the rest areas. Some dancers played dirty tricks, such as slipping sleeping pills into their opponents' drinks.

Finally, government doctors decided the dance marathons were dangerous to the dancers' health. Police began stopping the contests. The fad died out in the early 1930's.

A. Each question below asks you to use a context clue to help you determine the meaning of one of the new words used in the story on page 114. Put your answers on your paper.

1. Find **fad** in the story. What synonym for **fad** is used in the next sentence?
   a. dance
   b. marathon
   c. popular hobby

2. Find **marathon** in the story. What synonym for **marathon** is used in the next sentence?
   a. long contest
   b. couple
   c. record

3. An antonym in the sentence after the one that contains **zany** helps you know **zany** means __.
   a. few
   b. funny
   c. poor

4. If **spectators** watched the dancers, you know from experience that **spectators** are __.
   a. dancers
   b. viewers
   c. athletes

5. If dancers were **eliminated** from the contest for breaking rules, you know **eliminated** means __.
   a. removed
   b. praised
   c. added

6. Find **penalty** in the story. What synonym for **penalty** is used in the next sentence?
   a. legs
   b. prize
   c. punishment

7. The other words in the series with **jostled** help you know **jostled** means __.
   a. shoved
   b. kissed
   c. paid

8. The words right after **frayed** help you know that **frayed** means __.
   a. hard
   b. hurt
   c. strained

B. Look back at your answers in Activity A to find synonyms for the new words. On your paper, list the lesson words and their synonyms.

C. Write a sentence to answer each question below. Use the lesson word in dark type in your sentence.

1. Why do people often get **jostled** on a crowded dance floor?
2. How many **spectators** usually attend your school's basketball games?
3. Who is a performer on television who is very **zany**?

115

Here are the eight new words in this lesson. Their meanings are not listed. Look for the new words in the story below. Try to find context clues to help you define the lesson words. You will find some hints to help you in the questions on the next page.

artificial   guarantee
durable   techniques
avid   distribute
resorts   drawbacks

Making Snow

Everyone knows that people who ski must have snow. But now, skiers can still enjoy the sport, even when no snow has fallen. The skiers can use machine-made snow.

Actually, many skiers prefer **artificial** snow to the natural thing. Artificial snow is more **durable**, meaning it lasts longer. It is also harder and drier than natural snow. So skiers can race down the slopes at a faster speed.

Snow-making machines are used around the world. However, the demand for artificial snow is greatest in the eastern United States, where many **avid** skiers travel. These eager athletes vacation at ski **resorts** in Vermont, New Hampshire, and New York. The owners must promise their customers good snow conditions, or the skiers may go elsewhere. The snow-making machines **guarantee** that lots of snow will be around, even when nature doesn't provide the right amount.

How is artificial snow made? Basically, it is done by mixing cold water and air. The water and air are sprayed out of pipes. Almost immediately, the fine spray freezes into snow.

There are two **techniques** for spraying snow on the mountain slopes. One of the methods is to move the machines up and down the slopes, creating layers of snow cover. The other method is to make the snow in one big pile first. Then tractors are used to load, carry, and finally **distribute** the snow over the slopes.

Artificial snow has many advantages. But it also has **drawbacks**. Warm weather is the biggest problem. Above 32°F (0°C), the snow turns to slush. Also, strong winds can easily blow away the snow as it is made. To avoid this problem, snow sprayers shoot the snow in a low path to keep it under the wind. Artificial snow may not be perfect, but many skiers can't do without it.

A. Each question below asks you to use a context clue to help you determine the meaning of one of the new words used in the story on page 116. Put your answers on your paper.

1. An antonym used in the same sentence with **artificial** helps you know **artificial** means ___.
   a. natural
   b. not natural
   c. cold

2. The words right after **durable** help you know **durable** means ___.
   a. meaning
   b. artificial
   c. long-lasting

3. Find **avid** in the story. What synonym for **avid** is used in the next sentence?
   a. eager
   b. vacation
   c. athletes

4. From the way **resorts** is used, you can tell from experience that **resorts** are ___.
   a. machines
   b. stores
   c. vacation places

5. Find **guarantee** in the story. What synonym for **guarantee** is used in the sentence before?
   a. go
   b. promise
   c. know

6. Find **techniques** in the story. What synonym for **techniques** is used in the next sentence?
   a. slopes
   b. layers
   c. methods

7. The words in the series with **distribute** help you know **distribute** means ___.
   a. spread
   b. find
   c. make

8. Find **drawbacks** in the story. An antonym in the sentence before helps you know it means ___.
   a. advantages
   b. natural
   c. disadvantages

B. Look back at your answers in Activity A to find synonyms for the new words. On your paper, list the lesson words and their synonyms.

C. Write a sentence to answer each question below. Use the lesson word in dark type in your sentence.

1. Why is fruit made of wax or plastic called **artificial** fruit?
2. Which are more **durable**, wooden toys or plastic toys?
3. What do you think are some **drawbacks** of skiing?

Here are the eight new words in this lesson. Their meanings are not listed. Look for the new words in the story below. Try to find context clues to help you define the lesson words. You will find some hints to help you in the questions on the next page.

vocation	**revive**
severe	**massaged**
hasten	**rigorous**
navigate	**eligible**

EMT's Save Lives

Can you think and act quickly? Are you interested in a job in which something new happens every day? Are you looking for a **vocation** in which your quick thinking and acting can save lives? Then you might like to be an Emergency Medical Technician, or EMT.

When accidents occur, a team of EMT's is often the first help to arrive. An EMT is specially trained to give care and treatment to emergency victims at the scene of an accident or illness. The emergency may be anything from a **severe** accident to a minor cut.

EMT's learn about accidents over a special radio. They **hasten** to the scene, often in just a few minutes. The ambulance usually carries two EMT's and the driver. A fourth person helps **navigate**, or guide, the ambulance driver through heavy traffic.

At the scene, EMT's give the necessary care. In minor cases, a victim might need only a bandage. For a heart attack case, treatment may require mouth-to-mouth breathing to **revive** a person who has stopped breathing on his or her own. Or the chest of a victim whose heart has stopped beating may need to be **massaged**. As the chest is rubbed, the victim is rushed to a hospital.

Becoming an EMT requires long, thorough, and **rigorous** training. First, EMT's must take a 45-hour first-aid course. Afterward, they must take a more difficult 120-hour EMT course given by many police, fire, or health departments. This course includes spending time in a hospital emergency room to get firsthand experience. After completing the course, EMT's must pass a three-hour test to become **eligible**, or qualified, to get their EMT licenses.

To become an EMT, a person must be at least 18 and have a high school diploma. The job is exciting. It is also a good way to prepare for other medical careers, such as becoming a paramedic or a nurse.

A. Each question below asks you to use a context clue to help you determine the meaning of one of the new words used in the story on page 118. Put your answers on your paper.

1. Find **vocation** in the story. What synonym for **vocation** is used in the sentence before?
   a. day
   b. act
   c. job

2. An antonym used in the same sentence helps you know **severe** means ___.
   a. serious
   b. minor
   c. quick

3. If EMT's arrive at accidents in just a few minutes, you know **hasten** means ___.
   a. walk
   b. hurry
   c. listen

4. The words right after **navigate** help you know **navigate** means ___.
   a. drive
   b. announce
   c. guide

5. Since people need to breathe in order to live, you can guess that **revive** means ___.
   a. locate
   b. bring back to life
   c. help to see

6. Find **massaged** in the story. What word in the next sentence is a synonym of **massaged**?
   a. rushed
   b. rubbed
   c. stopped

7. The words in the series with **rigorous** help you know **rigorous** means ___.
   a. terrible
   b. thoughtful
   c. difficult

8. The words right after **eligible** help you know **eligible** means ___.
   a. necessary
   b. lucky
   c. qualified

B. Look back at your answers in Activity A to find synonyms for the new words. On your paper, list the lesson words and their synonyms.

C. Write a sentence to answer each question below. Use the lesson word in dark type in your sentence.

1. What are some other jobs that require **rigorous** training?
2. What do you need to do to be **eligible** for a driver's license?
3. What instrument helps sailors **navigate** a boat?

Here are the eight new words in this lesson. Their meanings are not listed. Look for the new words in the story below. Try to find context clues to help you define the lesson words. You will find some hints to help you in the questions on the next page.

inmates   **institutions**
stench   **banned**
reforms   **unsatisfactory**
asylums   **humane**

Dorothea Dix, Prison Reformer

In 1841, a Massachusetts school teacher named Dorothea Dix visited a jail to teach Sunday school to 20 women **inmates**. She was shocked by the way these prisoners were treated. They seemed hungry and neglected. Their rooms were small, cold, and crowded. Dorothea could barely stand the **stench** she smelled in the cells.

Dorothea discovered that the jail also held many insane people who couldn't afford to go to a hospital. These insane people were treated even worse than the criminals were.

Dorothea felt that great changes were needed. But before suggesting **reforms**, she decided to learn how other prisons and **asylums**, or homes for the insane, were run. She traveled throughout the country for five years. She visited hundreds of prisons, asylums, hospitals, and other **institutions**.

Dorothea found two different kinds of prisons in the United States. In one kind, prisoners were kept separate from each other at all times. In the other kind, inmates were allowed to work together, but talking together was **banned**.

Dorothea felt both systems were **unsatisfactory**. Neither one helped change criminals while they were in jail. Dorothea felt prisoners should be taught religion and the difference between right and wrong. She also felt prisoners should be taught useful skills.

Dorothea Dix continued working for prison reforms until her death at age 85. Her efforts paid off. Soon, new laws were passed. Insane people were put into asylums instead of prisons. Ministers and teachers were hired to teach religion and skills to inmates. Prison guards were trained to get along better with inmates. Because of Dorothea Dix, prisons have tried to become more **humane**, or caring, institutions.

A. Each question below asks you to use a context clue to help you determine the meaning of one of the new words used in the story on page 120. Put your answers on your paper.

1. Find **inmates** in the story. What word in the next sentence is a synonym for **inmates**?
   a. prisoners
   b. women
   c. jails

2. Since Dorothea smelled the **stench**, you can guess **stench** means —.
   a. people
   b. odor
   c. food

3. Find **reforms** in the story. What synonym for **reforms** is used in the sentence before?
   a. criminals
   b. changes
   c. decisions

4. The words right after **asylums** help you know **asylums** are —.
   a. places that need change
   b. places for criminals
   c. homes for the insane

5. The words in the series with **institutions** help you know **institutions** are —.
   a. public buildings
   b. houses
   c. illnesses

6. An antonym used in the same sentence helps you know **banned** means —.
   a. separated
   b. allowed
   c. not allowed

7. Since Dorothea did not like either system, you can tell **unsatisfactory** means —.
   a. not desirable
   b. not large
   c. excellent

8. The words right after **humane** help you know **humane** means —.
   a. crowded
   b. skillful
   c. caring

B. Look back at your answers in Activity A to find synonyms for the new words. On your paper, list the lesson words and their synonyms.

C. Write a sentence to answer each question below. Use the lesson word in dark type in your sentence.

1. What are some **reforms** that should be made in your school?
2. What actions are **banned** by the rules in your school?
3. How do teachers let students know if their work is **unsatisfactory**?

Here are 10 facts you have learned in Lessons 1–4 of Part 2. One word has been omitted from each fact sentence. Decide which choice listed below the sentence best fills the blank. Then write the completed sentences on your paper.

1. Many people took part in dance marathons, which were a __ in the United States during the 1920's and the early 1930's.
   penalty   location   fad

2. Hundreds of __ came out to watch couples try to dance for days and even weeks without stopping.
   dancers   spectators   dollars

3. Couples kept dancing until they were __ from the contest because their knees touched the floor.
   frayed   jostled   eliminated

4. Many skiers like the fact that artificial snow is more __ , or longer-lasting, than the natural thing.
   avid   durable   not natural

5. Snow-making machines help ski-resort owners __ that there will be snow on their slopes throughout the winter.
   guarantee   distribute   navigate

6. When accidents occur, Emergency Medical Technicians have to __ to the scene as fast as they can go.
   observe   hasten   navigate

7. Sometimes they must give mouth-to-mouth breathing to help __ a victim who has almost died.
   locate   revive   massage

8. To be __ to become an EMT, a person must take a lot of training and pass a special test.
   eligible   rigorous   severe

9. Dorothea Dix tried to bring about __ in the way things were done in U.S. prisons.
   asylums   institutions   reforms

10. Dorothea Dix helped to make sure that prisons treated inmates in a kinder, more __ way than they had before.
    rigorous   humane   unsatisfactory

Choose the word or phrase that means the same, or almost the same, as each word in dark type. Put your answers on your answer sheet. The test words come from Lessons 1 and 2.

Test Tips: Some answer choices are put in a test to trick you. Make sure you pick a synonym for the word in dark type. Don't pick an answer that fits in the phrase but is not a synonym of the test word.

1. receive a **penalty**
   a. present
   b. answer
   c. punishment
   d. prison

2. learn several **techniques**
   a. books
   b. methods
   c. words
   d. sports

3. **zany** actions
   a. funny
   b. slow
   c. dance
   d. popular

4. **distribute** the money
   a. locate
   b. spread
   c. earn
   d. conceal

5. **jostled** by the crowd
   a. hurt
   b. frightened
   c. lost
   d. shoved

6. one of the **spectators**
   a. victims
   b. dancers
   c. players
   d. viewers

7. an **avid** fan
   a. eager
   b. brilliant
   c. unhappy
   d. new

8. **frayed** nerves
   a. frightened
   b. strained
   c. open
   d. durable

9. recognize the **drawbacks**
   a. faces
   b. people
   c. information
   d. disadvantages

10. **artificial** fruit
   a. sweet
   b. natural
   c. not natural
   d. ripe

TAKING TESTS

Choose the word or phrase that means the same, or almost the same, as the word in dark type in each sentence below. Put your answers on your answer sheet. The test words come from Lessons 3 and 4.

Test Tips: Use the sentence context to help you. Try to put your answer choice in place of the word in dark type. Decide if the sentence still has the same meaning.

11. The apprentice was trying to become an expert at the new **vocation** — carpentry.
    a. building
    b. job
    c. office
    d. training

12. Smoking was **banned** within the school building.
    a. allowed
    b. noticed
    c. occurring
    d. not allowed

13. A compass helps sailors to **navigate** their ships.
    a. reach
    b. see
    c. guide
    d. sink

14. Learning to be a nurse requires **rigorous** training.
    a. difficult
    b. simple
    c. right
    d. quick

15. The man **massaged** his muscles to ease the pain.
    a. tightened
    b. removed
    c. calmed
    d. rubbed

16. Pets should receive **humane** treatment from their owners.
    a. painful
    b. swift
    c. caring
    d. personal

17. A **severe** heart attack can cause a person's death.
    a. serious
    b. minor
    c. fast
    d. qualified

18. The woman was overcome by the **stench** from the garbage dump.
    a. flowers
    b. odor
    c. people
    d. truck

Read the selection below. Notice the words in dark type. Choose the word or phrase that best answers each question below the selection.

Test Tips: Read the sentence that contains each test word carefully. Look for a context clue in that sentence or in the sentences near it. Make a logical guess about the test word's meaning. Then see if your guess is similar to one of the answers.

It usually takes four to six hours to fly across the Atlantic Ocean from the United States to France. In August 1978, it took three Americans six-and-a-half days to **traverse** the ocean. The three men made their flight in a way no one had ever done before — by balloon.

The three men — Ben Abruzzo, Maxie Anderson, and Larry Newman — **embarked** from Presque Island, Maine, on August 11 in a balloon **inflated** with helium. They arrived in a wheat field near Paris on August 18.

It was no simple flight. The balloonists had to **surmount**, or overcome, such dangers as storms, bitter-cold temperatures, and a dive that nearly proved deadly. The almost **fatal** dive occurred on the fifth day of the flight. The balloon floated into a cloud bank and dropped quickly from 22,000 feet to 4,000 feet. Fortunately, the sun broke through an opening, warming the balloon, and it rose again.

Two days later, the men landed the balloon near Paris. **Throngs** of French people greeted them. The crowds cheered wildly.

---

19. What does **traverse** mean in the selection?
   a. go across   c. notice
   b. locate   d. reach

20. What does **embarked** mean in the selection?
   a. came to   c. left
   b. tried   d. remained

21. What does **inflated** mean in the selection?
   a. clothed   c. touched
   b. announced   d. filled

22. What does **surmount** mean in the selection?
   a. fly   c. crash
   b. overcome   d. go across

23. What does **fatal** mean in the selection?
   a. cold   c. lucky
   b. safe   d. deadly

24. What does **throngs** mean in the selection?
   a. heroes   c. cheers
   b. crowds   d. voices

PART 3 *Words with Several Meanings*

The new words you are going to learn in Part 3 each have several different meanings. However, only one of the meanings will fit the way the word is used in a reading selection. You will be able to determine which meaning fits by using context clues to help you define the new words.

Look at the three pictures below. Each picture illustrates a different meaning of the same word. Can you guess what the secret word is? Do you know all the meanings of the word?

A single word can have several different meanings. You can find all of these meanings listed in a dictionary entry for the word. You need to look carefully at how the word is used in a sentence or paragraph to determine which meaning fits in your reading.

Look at the four sentences below. The word *trace* appears in each one. In each sentence, *trace* has a different meaning.

1. The detective was able to trace the criminal to his hideout.
2. Children often trace letters to help them learn script.
3. The flood left its trace on all the houses in the neighborhood.
4. The chef used only a trace of salt in the recipe.

Here are four different definitions of *trace*. Each meaning fits the way the word was used in one of the sentences you just read. On your paper, indicate which meaning fits in each sentence.

a. a small amount
b. pursue or follow
c. copy by following lines exactly
d. proof that something existed

Check your answers. Notice the way *trace* was used in each sentence. The correct matches are: 1. **b**, 2. **c**, 3. **d**, and 4. **a**.

Think about other words that have several different meanings. How many meanings can you think of for each of the following words? Write down your meanings. Then look up each word in a dictionary to find additional meanings.

bear
crown
deal
faint
log
match
name
pinch
stole

Do the activities on the next two pages. You will learn more about choosing the meaning of a word that fits in your reading.

A. Read the following paragraph about an unusual fact in the history of cars. Look at the way **early** is used in the paragraph. Try to decide what **early** means.

Ransom E. Olds was an **early** car inventor and manufacturer. He is the only person who has had two different types of cars named after him. One type was the Oldsmobile. The other was the Reo, named for his initials.

Here are two different meanings of **early**. Which one fits the way the word was used in the selection?

1. ahead of time
2. near the first or beginning

Check your answer. The meaning that fits in the story is **2**.

B. One word is printed in dark type in each sentence below about car history. Decide which meaning listed below the sentence fits the way the word in dark type is used. Put your answers on your paper.

1. In 1913, the Ford Motor Company was turning out 1,000 cars a day; today, approximately 5,500 cars are **assembled** each day.
   a. gathered in one place
   b. put together

2. Four different small-car models were **introduced** in 1960 — the Dart, the Corvair, the Falcon, and the Valiant.
   a. brought into use for the first time
   b. made someone known to others

3. The first truck to go across the United States was a three-ton Packard, which **managed** to complete the trip in 47 days in 1912.
   a. succeeded or was able
   b. controlled or directed

4. The first gasoline-powered car, made in 1885, was able to reach a top **rate** of 10 miles per hour.
   a. price or cost
   b. speed or pace

Check your answers. You should have picked **b** for 1, **a** for 2, **a** for 3, and **b** for 4.

C. Here are the kinds of questions you sometimes see on a reading test. Read the meaning printed at the top of each item. Then find the sentence in which the word in dark type has the same meaning. Put your answers on your paper.

1. hire for a job
   a. The new factory will **employ** 350 new workers.
   b. The detective needed to **employ** all of his skills to get out of the difficult situation.

2. circle or revolution
   a. The lights went out because of problems with the electrical **circuit**.
   b. The car made a complete **circuit** of the racetrack.

3. ring or peal
   a. We paid a $1.50 **toll** when we crossed the bridge.
   b. The church bells **toll** every Sunday morning.

4. welcome someone receives
   a. The soldier was given a warm **reception** when he came home.
   b. A large **reception** was held after the wedding.

5. safe from harm
   a. The secretary was able to **secure** a room for the meeting.
   b. I always feel more **secure** when my doors are locked.

6. surrender
   a. The defeated army was forced to **submit** to the enemy.
   b. Employees were asked to **submit** suggestions for improvement.

Check your answers. You should have picked **a** for 1, **b** for 2, **b** for 3, **a** for 4, **b** for 5, and **a** for 6.

Here are the eight new words in this lesson. Their meanings are not listed. Each lesson word has several different meanings. You will need to use context clues from the story below to help you determine the meaning that fits in the story.

dimension	elementary
craft	effort
illustrate	weather
apply	affords

Painting in a Big Way

Imagine painting a picture 100 or 200 feet wide. Walt Broyles has created paintings of that **dimension**. Broyles' work has been seen by millions of people, but few know about him or about his **craft**. That is because Broyles does his painting on billboards — large outdoor signs.

Today, most billboard painters use projectors to flash the pictures they are going to **illustrate** onto the billboards. They trace the drawings before they **apply** the paint. But Broyles is one of the few sign painters who does not trace first. Instead, he paints the entire sign freehand.

Painting billboards freehand is not an **elementary** task. The billboards, called "paints" or "bulletins" by sign painters, are usually about 15 feet high and 50 feet wide. It takes time and **effort** to paint the tall letters neatly. It also takes special skill to mix the oil paints properly for the picture part of the sign. Broyles and an assistant need about five days to complete an average-size billboard.

Broyles has painted some huge signs during his career. One of his

proudest achievements was a 200-foot-wide sign for a hotel. Another was a 100-foot-wide sign for a soft drink company. Unfortunately, both signs were blown down after a while. They were too big to **weather** strong winds.

Like other billboard painters, Broyles likes his work because it is done outdoors. The job also **affords** him the opportunity to travel from place to place. Broyles is in his 60's now, but he hopes to keep painting for many years to come.

A. Each of the new words in Lesson 1 is listed below. After each lesson word are two of its meanings. Decide which meaning fits the way the word was used in the story on pages 130–131. Put your answers on your paper.

1. dimension
   a. measurement or size
   b. aspect or part

2. craft
   a. boat or plane
   b. art

3. illustrate
   a. give an example
   b. draw or paint

4. apply
   a. put on
   b. fit or be relevant

5. elementary
   a. beginning
   b. simple

6. effort
   a. attempt
   b. hard work

7. weather
   a. endure or bear
   b. climate

8. affords
   a. provides
   b. is able to pay for

B. The words below are synonyms of four of the new words in this lesson. Write down the lesson word that matches each synonym.

1. draw
2. simple
3. provides
4. art

C. Write a sentence to answer each question below. Use the lesson word in dark type in your sentence.

1. Which requires more **effort**, drawing freehand or tracing?
2. Which has greater **dimension**, a billboard or a wall poster?
3. What tools can people use to **apply** paint?

Here are the eight new words in this lesson. Their meanings are not listed. Each lesson word has several different meanings. You will need to use context clues from the story below to help you determine the meaning that fits in the story.

scores	**discrimination**
figures	**associates**
manage	**residence**
blaze	**mounts**

Black Cowboys, Yesterday and Today

You have probably seen **scores** of movies and television shows about cowboys. But you probably don't know that many of those tough, hard-riding **figures** were black men. As many as 5,000 black cowboys helped to build the Old West.

The first black cowboys came to the West as slaves of ranchers in Texas. There, they learned to **manage** herds of cattle and to do other ranch chores. After the Civil War, the slaves were freed. Most decided to continue at the jobs they knew best. Like whites, they were hired to tame wild horses and to lead cattle herds north to markets. A typical team driving cattle north consisted of eight cowboys, two of whom were black. The black cowboys also helped to **blaze** new trails through areas in the West that had not been explored before.

Very little has been written about the black cowboys. One of the cowboys did write an autobiography in 1907. His name was Nat Love. In his book, Love described the brave and dangerous life he had led.

The black cowboys did face some **discrimination** because of their color. But, in general, they were treated as equals to their white **associates**. They received

132

equal wages and worked, slept, and ate with their white companions.

Today, there are still several thousand black cowboys who work on ranches or take part in rodeos. Not all of these cowboys have their **residence** in the West. Some live in large Eastern cities. In New York, a group of black cowboys ride their **mounts** each Saturday in one of the city's parks. Sometimes they even ride through the streets of the city. They show children rope tricks and answer their questions. Most of the children, and many adults, are seeing real-life cowboys for the first time.

A. Each of the new words in Lesson 2 is listed below. After each lesson word are two of its meanings. Decide which meaning fits the way the word was used in the story on pages 132–133. Put your answers on your paper.

1. scores
   a. point totals
   b. many or lots

2. figures
   a. people
   b. numbers

3. manage
   a. succeed in doing something
   b. control or handle

4. blaze
   a. open up or explore
   b. burn brightly

5. discrimination
   a. prejudice
   b. ability to choose carefully

6. associates
   a. companions
   b. connects

7. residence
   a. time of medical training
   b. home

8. mounts
   a. horses
   b. mountains

B. The words below are synonyms of four of the new words in this lesson. Write down the lesson word that matches each synonym.

1. prejudice
2. control

3. companions
4. people

C. Write a sentence to answer each question below. Use the lesson word in dark type in your sentence.

1. On which street is your **residence**?
2. What actor or actress has been in **scores** of television shows?
3. Who was one explorer who tried to **blaze** trails into an unknown part of the United States?

Here are the 10 new words in this lesson. Their meanings are not listed. Each lesson word has several different meanings. You will need to use context clues from the story below to help you determine the meaning that fits in the story.

occupied	dismiss
import	assume
producer	value
partial	evidence
dedication	degree

Japan's Rise to the Top

Japan is only about the size of the state of Montana. Yet more than 120 million people live in that country. That is half the U.S. population. Most of the people live along the coast, since 85 percent of Japan is **occupied** by mountains. Japan is the world's most crowded nation.

In addition, the Japanese have almost no natural resources. They **import** nearly all of their oil and coal. Since most land is too hilly for farming, Japan must also bring in about a third of its food.

Despite all of these needs, Japan is a world leader in industry. How is this possible? Part of the answer is modern factories built after World War II. These factories have helped Japan become the world's leading **producer** of steel, watches, cameras, and automobiles.

But modern factories are only a **partial** explanation for Japan's success. The other part is the special **dedication**, or devotion, that the Japanese show toward the companies for which they work.

There is a good reason for this spirit. Japanese companies take good care of workers and their families. They rarely **dismiss** workers. The companies **assume** all costs for health care. They also provide free recreation after work and on weekends.

Working hard is an important **value** to the Japanese. People come to work early and leave late. In this way, they show **evidence** of their love for the company. Many Japanese workers also start their day by singing a song about the greatness of their company.

Japan's progress has produced some problems, however. Cities are overcrowded with people and cars. There is also a high **degree** of air and water pollution. The Japanese are sure they can solve these problems through the same kind of hard work and caring that has helped them become world leaders.

A. Each of the new words in Lesson 3 is listed below. After each lesson word are two of its meanings. Decide which meaning fits the way the word was used in the story on page 134. Put your answers on your paper.

1. **occupied**
   a. covered or filled
   b. busy

2. **import**
   a. importance
   b. bring in

3. **producer**
   a. person in charge of a play or movie
   b. manufacturer or maker

4. **partial**
   a. favoring or liking
   b. part or incomplete

5. **dedication**
   a. devotion
   b. inscription in a book

6. **dismiss**
   a. fire or release
   b. give permission to leave

7. **assume**
   a. think or believe
   b. take charge of

8. **value**
   a. principle or belief
   b. worth

9. **evidence**
   a. proof
   b. testimony in court

10. **degree**
   a. college diploma
   b. level or amount

B. The words below are synonyms of four of the new words in this lesson. Write down the lesson word that matches each synonym.

1. devotion
2. level
3. principle
4. release

C. Write a sentence to answer each question below. Use the lesson word in dark type in your sentence.

1. What is one way you can show **evidence** that you have good school spirit?
2. What are some products that the United States **imports** from Japan?
3. How much of your state is **occupied** by mountains?

Here are 10 facts you have learned in Lessons 1–3 of Part 3. The words in italics in the fact sentences are synonyms for the 10 lesson words listed below. Rewrite the sentences, using the lesson words to replace their synonyms.

1. Walt Broyles paints signs of a huge *size* for outdoor billboards.

2. Broyles is one of the few sign painters who still *draw* their pictures freehand.

3. Painting a 100-foot-wide sign freehand requires a great deal of time and *hard work*.

4. Black cowboys helped to *explore* new trails in the Old West.

5. In general, black cowboys were treated as equals to their white *companions* on ranches and cattle drives.

6. Some black cowboys today have their *homes* in large cities in the East, such as New York.

7. Japan is a leading producer of manufactured products, even though it must *bring in* most of its fuel and much of its food.

8. Japanese workers show a strong *devotion* toward their companies.

9. Japanese companies seldom *fire* workers, and most people work for the same company all of their lives.

10. Japanese workers show *proof* of their love of their companies by coming to work early and leaving late.

LESSON WORDS

import	illustrate
associates	evidence
effort	residences
dedication	dimension
blaze	dismiss

Choose the sentence in which the word in dark type means the same as the definition given. Put your answers on your answer sheet.

Test Tips: Try to substitute the definition for the word in dark type in each sentence. Then see which sentence makes sense. Don't be tricked by a different meaning of the same word.

1. amount
   a. The temperature was −1 **degree** this morning.
   b. The injured man felt a high **degree** of pain.
   c. The ship's course was shifted one **degree** west.

2. principle or belief
   a. This ring's **value** is $5,000.
   b. If you **value** your time, don't waste it on foolish things.
   c. Getting a good education is an important **value** in my family.

3. people
   a. Jefferson and Adams are key **figures** in U.S. history.
   b. My mother can add a row of **figures** quickly.
   c. The football game **figures** to be a close contest.

4. lots or many
   a. The team made six **scores** in the game.
   b. **Scores** of workers left the building at 5 p.m.
   c. That man has lived four **score** years.

5. control or handle
   a. Can you **manage** to get to class on time?
   b. My mother was asked to **manage** the new store.
   c. I will **manage** to see the boss about a raise.

6. put on
   a. Always clean a wall before you **apply** paint.
   b. That answer does not **apply** in this situation.
   c. I will **apply** for a store credit card.

7. take charge of
   a. I **assume** my father will meet me at the station.
   b. He will **assume** a deep voice to sound older.
   c. The company will **assume** all insurance costs.

8. endure
   a. The tree was unable to **weather** the high winds.
   b. The **weather** was warm and humid.
   c. In time, raw wood will **weather** and turn darker.

PART 4 *Word Parts*

In Part 4, you are going to learn another method for guessing what a new word means. You will learn to look at parts of an unfamiliar word to see if the parts can give you a clue to the word's overall meaning. Sometimes part of a new word will be a word you already know. Sometimes a word has special parts added at the beginning or at the end — prefixes and suffixes. You will learn to use these word parts as meaning clues.

Look at the two pictures below. One picture illustrates the meaning of the word **victorious**. The other picture illustrates the meaning of the word **motionless**. Can you match each picture with the right word? On your paper, write your guess about each word's meaning.

Sometimes you will see an unfamiliar word in your reading or on a vocabulary test. You may notice that you can spot a word you already know within the new word. Many times you can use the word inside, called the *base word*, to help you determine what the new word means.

Another way to use word parts as clues is to look at prefixes or suffixes added to a base word. One prefix you often see on words is *mis*. The words *misunderstand* and *mislead* have this prefix. The prefix *mis* means "incorrectly." So *misunderstand* means "understand something incorrectly." What would *mislead* probably mean?

Two suffixes you often see added to base words are *ous* and *ful*. The words *joyous* and *skillful* have these endings. The two suffixes have the same meaning, "filled with" or "having." So *joyous* means "filled with joy." What would *skillful* probably mean?

Read the following true story about a famous first. Three words are printed in dark type. Use word parts to help guess their meanings.

In 1843, Sir Henry Cole was **desirous** of saying Merry Christmas in a new way. He asked the artist John Collcott Horsley to design a drawing **suitable** for a holiday greeting. Cole had 1,000 copies of the drawing printed on paper and sent them to his friends. These holiday greetings were the first Christmas cards. Most of the cards have since been destroyed or **misplaced**. Only 12 are known to exist today.

An early British Christmas card.

---

1. The base word and suffix of **desirous** help you guess it means ___.
   a. having desire or wanting   b. filled with worry

2. The base word of **suitable** helps you know it means ___.
   a. beautiful   b. fitting

3. The base word and prefix of **misplaced** help you guess it means ___.
   a. sold for a high price   b. lost or put in the wrong place

Check your answers. Correct answers are **a** for 1, **b** for 2, and **b** for 3.

A. Look at the words in List 1 below. Try to find a base word you already know inside each new word. Notice any prefixes or suffixes. Match each new word with its meaning in List 2. Put your answers on your paper.

LIST 1
1. prolong
2. misshapen
3. frightful
4. courageous
5. profitable

LIST 2
a. scary
b. money-making
c. badly shaped
d. lengthen
e. brave

Check your answers. You should have chosen **d** for 1, **c** for 2, **a** for 3, **e** for 4, and **b** for 5.

B. Read the following paragraph about another famous first event. Look for word parts in the words in dark type. Then answer the questions at the top of page 141. Put your answers on your paper.

The first comic book was created in 1933. Its size, glossy cover, and **format** in story panels were similar to today's comics. At first, comic books were **reprints** of newspaper comic strips. Then, in 1938, *Action Comics* came out. *Superman* and comics about other **forceful** heroes soon followed. By 1943, *Superman*'s **readership** was so large that 1.5 million copies were sold each month. People who agreed to throw away their old comics were **misled**. The first issue of *Action Comics* is now worth $5,000.

1. Which word means "people who read something"?
2. Which word means "strong" or "having force"?
3. Which word means "copies of things already printed"?
4. Which word means "led into an error in thinking"?
5. Which word means "form" or "arrangement"?

Check your answers. Your answers should be 1. readership, 2. forceful, 3. reprints, 4. misled, and 5. format.

C. Here are the kinds of questions you sometimes see on reading tests. Read each incomplete sentence below. Then find the answer that best completes the sentence. Look for base words and other word parts to help you choose your answers. Put your answers on your paper.

1. A **hateful** person is not ___.
   a. hungry
   b. loving
   c. annoying

2. If you **misbehave**, you act ___.
   a. nicely
   b. alone
   c. badly

3. If you are **empty-handed**, you are carrying ___.
   a. a heavy weight
   b. a small package
   c. nothing

4. A **healthful** activity is ___.
   a. good for you
   b. bad for you
   c. dangerous

5. A **puzzlement** is something that is ___.
   a. sweet
   b. confusing
   c. loud

Check your answers. You should have picked **b** for 1, **c** for 2, **c** for 3, **a** for 4, and **b** for 5.

Here are the eight new words in this lesson. Their meanings are not listed. Notice how the words are used in the story below. Also pay close attention to base words, prefixes, and suffixes. They will help you define the new words.

homeowners   plentiful
enable   popularity
attraction   affordable
advantageous   advancements

Television by the Dish

Some people take their television viewing seriously. They own TV sets with screens as large as six feet across. They also have machines to make and play recordings of their favorite programs.

Now, a small but growing number of **homeowners** are also buying a new television-related product called a "receiving dish." The dish measures from 10 to 20 feet across. Owners usually set them up in their backyards. The dishes **enable** viewers to bring in TV signals from as many as 70 channels from all over the world.

The dish receives signals from many man-made satellites circling the earth. Owners select their channels by aiming the dish at the satellite of their choice.

Many people in the U.S. have receiving dishes. Most have paid from $5,000 to $20,000 for the equipment. The dishes' main **attraction** seems to be sports. A dish allows viewers to see games they might miss otherwise. A California dish owner watches hockey games broadcast by a New York station. One man in Florida even watched the 1980 Olympic games beamed from Moscow.

Receiving dishes are **advantageous** to other viewers besides sports fans. Right now, many country dwellers can tune in only one or two TV stations. Often the picture is poor. The dish offers these people a **plentiful** range of clear TV broadcasts.

In the future, the increasing **popularity** of receiving dishes will probably drive down their cost. They may soon cost as little as $100 to $250. Then even more people will find them **affordable**. New scientific **advancements** may also allow smaller dishes to be created that will do the same work as the large models now in use.

A. Look for word parts in the lesson words on page 142 to help you pick the best meanings in the questions below. Put your answers on your paper.

1. The two words you see inside **homeowners** help you know it means ___.
   a. people who watch TV
   b. people who sell houses
   c. people who own houses

2. The base word of **enable** helps you know it means ___.
   a. make able or possible
   b. make impossible
   c. make unhappy

3. The base word of **attraction** helps you know it means ___.
   a. beauty
   b. lure
   c. part

4. The base word and suffix of **advantageous** help you know it means ___.
   a. enjoyable
   b. helpful
   c. expensive

5. The base word almost spelled out in **plentiful** and its suffix help you know it means ___.
   a. small or tiny
   b. excellent or fine
   c. large or many

6. The base word of **popularity** helps you know it means ___.
   a. favor or appeal
   b. size or dimension
   c. cost

7. The base word of **affordable** helps you know it means ___.
   a. able to be seen
   b. able to be taught
   c. able to be bought

8. The base word of **advancements** helps you know it means ___.
   a. equipment
   b. improvements
   c. workers

B. Write a sentence to answer each question below. Use the lesson word in dark type in your sentence.

1. What is one reason for the **popularity** of television?
2. Why is having an antenna **advantageous** to TV viewers?
3. Why aren't receiving dishes **affordable** to most TV viewers today?

LESSON 2

Here are the 10 new words in this lesson. Their meanings are not listed. Notice how the words are used in the story below. Also pay close attention to base words, prefixes, and suffixes. They will help you define the new words.

outsiders	expansion
overpopulated	mindful
misjudge	heightened
retirees	doubtful
spacious	mistrust

Western Overgrowth

In the early 1970's, Oregon's Governor Tom McCall asked **outsiders** to stop moving to Oregon. McCall was concerned that the West would soon become as **overpopulated** as the East already was. People laughed at McCall. However, now it is clear that the governor did not **misjudge** the growing trend in the Western United States.

Between 1970 and 1980, the population of the Western states increased three times faster than that of the rest of the country. Job opportunities in Texas and Colorado attracted many people looking for work. Huge corporations in these states encouraged new workers to come west. Better climate and clean air attracted scores of **retirees** to Arizona, New Mexico, and Utah. These people decided to spend their later years in the large, **spacious** surroundings of the Western states.

The **expansion** of the West happened almost too quickly. Longtime Western residents are **mindful** that some difficult problems may result from this rapid growth.

One concern is water. Having enough water has always been a problem in the West. The growth in population has **heightened** this problem. Conserving water may help, but experts are **doubtful** that there will be enough water for everyone.

Increases in crime have also occurred. Small Western towns not used to crime have been hit by crime waves. Residents of some towns have begun to **mistrust** strangers.

Many people went west to avoid problems such as overcrowding and crime. Now, they are worried that these problems may have moved west along with them.

144

A. Look for word parts in the lesson words on page 144 to help you pick the best meanings in the questions below. Put your answers on your paper.

1. The beginning of **outsiders** helps you know it means __.
   a. friends
   b. strangers
   c. criminals

2. The base word and beginning of **overpopulated** help you know it means __.
   a. overcrowded
   b. empty
   c. too popular

3. The base word and prefix of **misjudge** help you know it means __.
   a. lose
   b. observe carefully
   c. guess incorrectly

4. The base word of **retirees** helps you know it means __.
   a. people who are tired
   b. people who have retired
   c. young people

5. The base word and suffix of **spacious** help you know it means __.
   a. small or tiny
   b. open or large
   c. beautiful or lovely

6. The base word nearly spelled out in **expansion** helps you know it means __.
   a. growth
   b. discovery
   c. climate

7. The base word and suffix of **mindful** help you know it means __.
   a. seeing
   b. aware
   c. unsure

8. The base word of **heightened** helps you know it means __.
   a. increased
   b. upset
   c. dried up

9. The base word and suffix of **doubtful** help you know it means __.
   a. certain
   b. uncertain
   c. hopeful

10. The base word and prefix of **mistrust** help you know it means __.
    a. love
    b. be kind to
    c. be suspicious of

B. Write a sentence to answer each question below. Use the lesson word in dark type in your sentence.

1. What is the most **spacious** room in your school?
2. What modern invention has **heightened** the problem of air pollution?
3. What city has gone through a great **expansion** in recent years?

For the items below, choose the word or phrase that best completes each sentence. Put your answers on your answer sheet.

Test Tips: This type of question asks you to think about the meaning of the key word. Then you need to use that meaning to help you choose the best answer. Read the incomplete sentences carefully. Use word parts to help you guess the meaning of each key word.

1. A spacious building is one that is __.
   a. cold and dark
   b. old and broken down
   c. tiny and crowded
   d. large and roomy

2. If you mistrust people in a store, you would __.
   a. shop there a lot
   b. not shop there
   c. want a job there
   d. tell friends to shop there

3. If a product is affordable to most people, it is probably __.
   a. not very expensive
   b. very expensive
   c. very small
   d. very large

4. Most retirees are people who are __.
   a. young
   b. famous
   c. old
   d. strangers

5. A candidate who has the most popularity will probably __.
   a. lose an election
   b. win an election
   c. drop out of an election
   d. not run for office

6. If jobs are plentiful in a company, __.
   a. few people will be hired
   b. no one will be hired
   c. many people will be hired
   d. two people will be hired

7. If advancements are made in a neighborhood, things will usually __.
   a. get worse
   b. remain the same
   c. start getting worse
   d. improve

8. The main attraction at a circus is something __.
   a. no one wants to see
   b. no one can find
   c. everyone wants to see
   d. everyone has forgotten

UNIT III
STUDY SKILLS

PART 1: *Visual Materials*   148

PART 2: *Reference Skills*   174

PART 1 *Visual Materials*

You can get facts in many different ways:

A. By reading a passage.

Together the Great Lakes are the largest body of fresh water in the world. Of the five lakes, only one is entirely inside the borders of the United States. That is Lake Michigan. The other four Great Lakes are shared by the U.S. and Canada. They are Lake Erie, Lake Huron, Lake Superior, and Lake Ontario. The largest of these lakes is Lake Superior and the smallest one is Lake Ontario.

B. By looking at maps. (Maps are drawings of parts of the world.)

C. By reading a chart called a table. (A table is a list of facts.)

LENGTHS OF THE GREAT LAKES	
Name	**Length (in miles)**
Lake Superior	350
Lake Michigan	307
Lake Erie	241
Lake Huron	206
Lake Ontario	193

D. By looking at a graph where the facts really stand out.

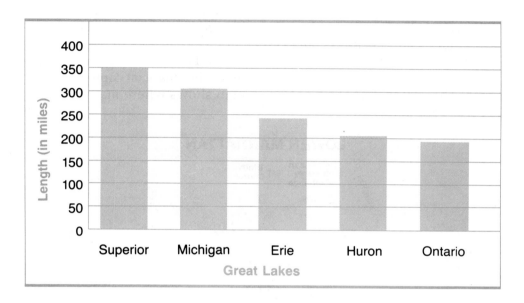

Read the questions below. They are based on the visual materials you just studied. See if you can answer these questions. Write your answers on your paper.

1. Which visual material gives the exact number of miles of Lake Erie?
  a. passage   c. table
  b. map   d. graph

2. Which visual material shows the location of Lake Michigan in the United States?
  a. passage   c. table
  b. map   d. graph

3. Which visual material shows that Lake Superior is longer than Lake Michigan?
  a. passage   c. table
  b. map   d. graph

4. Which visual material tells that the Great Lakes make up the largest body of fresh water in the world?
  a. passage   c. table
  b. map   d. graph

The Tip of Manhattan

The Dutch people settled on the tip of Manhattan Island in New York in the year 1625. They soon cleared the land for farms. Today, Lower Manhattan is famous for its tall skyscrapers. Few visitors to New York soon forget the beautiful New York skyline of Lower Manhattan.

Lower Manhattan is also famous for being the financial capital of the world. This street map of Lower Manhattan shows where many important buildings are.

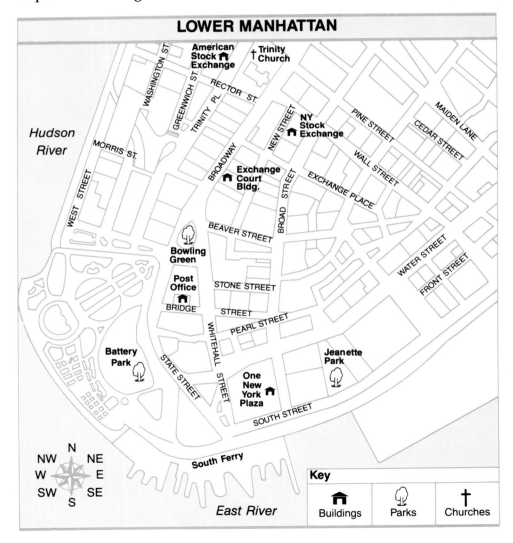

At the bottom of the map are a map key and a compass rose. The key shows the symbols used on the map, such as parks. The compass rose shows the directions in which the streets run: north (N), south (S), east (E), west (W), northeast (NE), northwest (NW), southeast (SE), and southwest (SW).

Use the map on page 150 to answer these questions. Choose the best answer.

1. What street borders Battery Park on the east?
   a. Broadway
   b. State Street
   c. Wall Street
   d. Water Street

Check your answer. The symbol 🌳 stands for park. Find Battery Park and look at the streets to the right (east) of it. The answer is **b**.

2. You walk on Broadway from Bowling Green toward Trinity Church. In what direction are you walking?
   a. northeast
   b. southwest
   c. southeast
   d. west

3. You are at Broad and Wall streets. You want to go to Pearl Street. In what direction would you walk?
   a. east
   b. north
   c. south
   d. west

4. You're at South Ferry. What is the fastest way to walk to Trinity Church?
   a. Whitehall Street to Broadway
   b. State Street to Broadway
   c. South Street to Wall Street
   d. Trinity Place

5. What park is north of the Post Office?
   a. Battery Park
   b. Jeanette Park
   c. Bowling Green
   d. none of the above

6. The New York Stock Exchange is between which two streets?
   a. Pearl and Water
   b. South and State
   c. Wall and Exchange
   d. State and Pearl

7. The American Stock Exchange is located ___ of Trinity Church.
   a. west
   b. north
   c. south
   d. east

8. Looking south from One New York Plaza, you'll see ___.
   a. Broadway
   b. the East River
   c. Pine Street
   d. Wall Street

Valley Forge

The army was on the run. They stopped at Valley Forge. There, General George Washington and his troops camped during the winter of 1777–1778. It was the time of the Revolutionary War.

That winter in Valley Forge was long and harsh. Many soldiers died. But General Washington and his troops did not lose their courage. In the spring they continued their fight for American independence. They won.

The map below shows the Valley Forge area as it looks today.

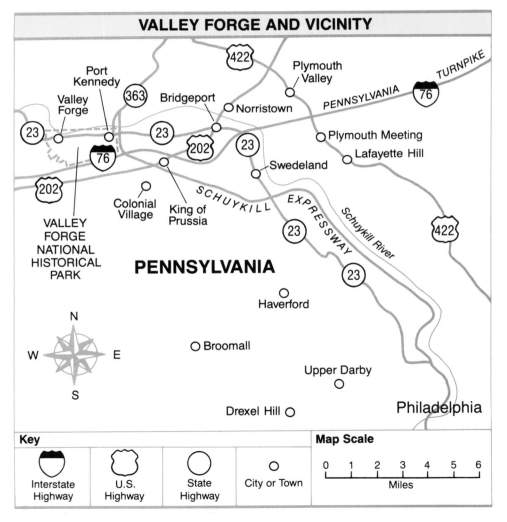

VALLEY FORGE AND VICINITY

Look at the map scale. You can use it to find the distance from one place to another. Perhaps you want to know how far Swedeland is from Lafayette Hill. Place a piece of paper on the map so the edge touches both cities. Put one dot on the paper at Swedeland and one at Lafayette Hill. Now place the paper along the scale. One dot should be on 0. The other will be at the 4-mile mark. So, Lafayette Hill is about 4 miles from Swedeland.

Use the map on page 152 to answer these questions. Choose the best answer.

1. What is the distance on U.S. Highway 422 between Lafayette Hill and Plymouth Meeting?
   a. about 1½ miles
   b. about 3 miles
   c. about 100 miles
   d. about 11 miles

Check your answer. The distance between Lafayette Hill and Plymouth Meeting along U.S. Highway 422 is about 1½ miles. The answer is **a.**

2. Which highway is between Bridgeport and Norristown?
   a. Interstate Highway 202
   b. U.S. Highway 202
   c. State Highway 23
   d. U.S. Highway 23

3. Interstate Highway 76 is also called the ___.
   a. King of Prussia Road
   b. Schuykill Expressway
   c. Interstate 422
   d. Pennsylvania Turnpike

4. What is the direction from King of Prussia to Philadelphia along the Schuykill Expressway?
   a. northeast
   b. northwest
   c. southeast
   d. southwest

5. What is the distance between Bridgeport and Norristown?
   a. 1 mile
   b. 5 miles
   c. 23 miles
   d. 10 miles

6. What town is about 2 miles west of Port Kennedy on State Highway 23?
   a. Philadelphia
   b. King of Prussia
   c. Bridgeport
   d. Valley Forge

7. How far is Bridgeport from Port Kennedy along State Highway 23.
   a. about 4 miles
   b. about 1 mile
   c. about 2½ miles
   d. about 5½ miles

LESSON 3

Number One

An American Indian named Squanto introduced the Pilgrims to it in 1621. Today it is the largest crop in the United States. People eat it at breakfast, lunch, and dinner. But it is mainly used to feed beef cattle, hogs, sheep, chickens, and dairy cows. What is it? Maize. It is also known as corn.

The U.S. produces almost half the corn grown in the world. Most of the corn is grown in the North Central states. The map below shows where corn and many other products are found in the North Central states.

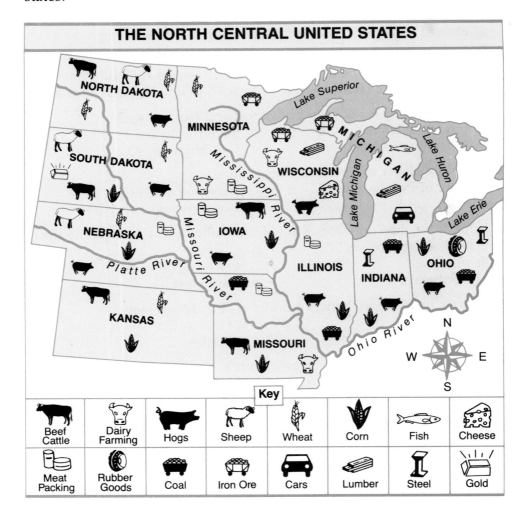

THE NORTH CENTRAL UNITED STATES

Key

| Beef Cattle | Dairy Farming | Hogs | Sheep | Wheat | Corn | Fish | Cheese |
| Meat Packing | Rubber Goods | Coal | Iron Ore | Cars | Lumber | Steel | Gold |

154

A product map is a special type of map. It shows where the chief crops, minerals, and manufactured goods are produced. The map key shows what the symbols on the map represent.

Use the map on page 154 to answer these questions. Choose the best answer.

1. In what state is gold produced?
a. South Dakota
b. Missouri
c. Michigan
d. North Dakota

Check your answer. The symbol for gold is shown within the borders of South Dakota. The answer is **a**.

2. What two states manufacture steel?
a. Wisconsin and Ohio
b. Iowa and Michigan
c. Ohio and Indiana
d. Minnesota and Iowa

3. Most fishing is done in which state?
a. Wisconsin
b. Ohio
c. Michigan
d. Minnesota

4. In how many states is coal produced?
a. twelve
b. three
c. four
d. seven

5. Which product is not produced in North Dakota, Minnesota, and Wisconsin?
a. lumber
b. wheat
c. hogs
d. corn

6. Which two products come only from Michigan?
a. fish and iron ore
b. lumber and cars
c. fish and cars
d. lumber and cheese

7. Which product is produced in most states west of the Mississippi River?
a. wheat
b. coal
c. steel
d. lumber

8. Both states that produce lumber border on ___.
a. Lake Erie
b. Lake Michigan
c. the Missouri River
d. the Ohio River

Rain and Crops

Without rain, crops could not grow. Fortunately, long droughts do not happen very often in the United States. The normal amount of rainfall the United States gets each year makes the U.S. one of the leading agricultural producers in the world.

Most of the food in the U.S. is grown in the Great Plains region. Many types of crops are grown, from wheat to strawberries. Why are certain crops grown in some places and not in others? To answer this question, look at the maps below.

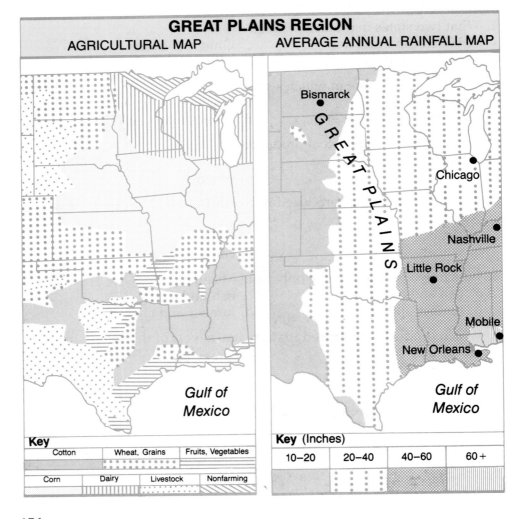

GREAT PLAINS REGION

AGRICULTURAL MAP   AVERAGE ANNUAL RAINFALL MAP

156

Compare the agricultural and rainfall maps of the Great Plains region on page 156. You will see how the rainfall patterns affect the crops that are grown.

Use the two maps to answer the questions below. Choose the best answer.

1. The major corn-growing area has an average rainfall of about __.
   a. 10–20 inches
   b. 20–40 inches
   c. 40–60 inches
   d. 60–80 inches

Check your answer. The symbol ⬜ is shown in the center of the map. That area gets about 20–40 inches of rain per year. The answer is **b**.

2. What products are grown along the Gulf of Mexico?
   a. fruits and vegetables
   b. corn
   c. cotton
   d. wheats and grains

3. Which of these cities usually gets the most rainfall each year?
   a. Chicago
   b. Mobile
   c. Bismarck
   d. Nashville

4. How many inches of rainfall does Chicago usually get each year?
   a. 10–20 inches
   b. 20–40 inches
   c. 40–60 inches
   d. over 60 inches

5. New Orleans would be a good place to get __.
   a. dairy products
   b. wheat and grains
   c. fruits and vegetables
   d. corn

6. What is the average rainfall in places where dairy products come from?
   a. 10–20 inches
   b. 20–40 inches
   c. 40–60 inches
   d. over 60 inches

7. What grows in areas that get an average of 10–20 inches of rain?
   a. grains and livestock
   b. cotton and corn
   c. fruit and vegetables
   d. wheat and fruit

8. Which statement is true?
   a. Corn would probably not grow in Mobile.
   b. Wheat only grows in Bismarck.
   c. Corn would not grow in Chicago.
   d. Cotton grows only in Little Rock.

Then and Now

Would you believe that the first recorded automobile trip across the United States took 10 weeks? That trip from San Francisco, California, to New York City began May 23, 1903, and ended August 1, 1903. The distance is only 3,025 miles. But the roads and the cars of 1903 weren't what they are today. If you were to make that same trip today by car, it would take you less than one week. And if you made that same trip across the country by plane, it would take only a few hours. Times certainly have changed.

The mileage chart below shows the road miles between different cities in America.

ROAD MILES BETWEEN U.S. CITIES

FROM TO	New York	Chicago	St. Louis	Boston	San Francisco	Pittsburgh
	Miles	Miles	Miles	Miles	Miles	Miles
Atlanta	855	695	558	1,068	2,523	697
Baltimore	187	687	817	399	2,876	230
Boston	216	975	1,178	—	3,163	508
Chicago	843	—	291	975	2,189	461
Cincinnati	659	295	338	876	2,402	284
Denver	1,851	1,016	856	1,989	1,270	1,482
Detroit	667	275	543	699	2,458	285
Houston	1,636	1,085	794	1,916	1,955	1,319
Kansas City	1,319	499	252	1,456	1,874	937
Los Angeles	2,915	2,095	1,848	3,052	403	2,533
New Orleans	1,325	925	695	1,536	2,303	1,093
New York	—	843	966	216	3,025	388
Philadelphia	92	762	885	304	2,944	305
San Francisco	3,025	2,189	2,126	3,163	—	2,648
Washington, DC	225	687	801	437	2,869	230

A table is arranged in columns and rows, which all have labels. A column is read from top to bottom. A row is read from left to right.

A mileage chart is a special table. Each column and row names a place. To find the distance between two places, locate one name in a column and the other in a row. The number where the column and the row meet is the number of miles between the two places.

Use the table on page 158 to answer these questions. Choose the best answer.

1. What is the distance from Chicago to Baltimore?
  a. 695 miles
  b. 187 miles
  c. 687 miles
  d. 1,000 miles

Check your answer. Find the column labeled Chicago. Find the row labeled Baltimore. They meet at the number 687. The answer is **c.**

2. How far is Boston from Atlanta?
  a. 1,068 miles
  b. 855 miles
  c. 437 miles
  d. 3 miles

3. Pittsburgh and Philadelphia are cities in Pennsylvania. How many miles apart are the two cities?
  a. 92
  b. 610
  c. 386
  d. 305

4. About how many miles are there between St. Louis and Chicago?
  a. fewer than 200
  b. fewer than 300
  c. more than 300
  d. more than 500

5. Which of these cities is farthest from St. Louis?
  a. Boston
  b. Los Angeles
  c. New York
  d. New Orleans

6. Which two cities are almost the same distance from Pittsburgh?
  a. Cincinnati and Boston
  b. Los Angeles and Detroit
  c. Detroit and Houston
  d. Cincinnati and Detroit

7. Which major cities are less than 300 miles from Washington, DC?
  a. New York and Chicago
  b. New York and Pittsburgh
  c. Boston and St. Louis
  d. San Francisco and Pittsburgh

8. You drive from New York to Boston. The next day you drive on to Chicago. What is the total number of miles you have driven?
  a. 843
  b. 975
  c. 216
  d. 1,191

Power for the Future

Each year, Americans use more and more energy. It is used to heat and light homes, and to run cars. Today, the United States imports a large part of the energy used. Energy experts say that about half of the energy needed in the U. S. will be imported by the mid-1980's. That means 50 percent of the energy will come from U.S. resources.

What kind of energy should be developed? Some people feel it should be nuclear power. Others feel the U.S. should develop non-nuclear energy, such as solar power.

The bar graph below shows the estimated percentages of kinds of energy that will come from U.S. resources by the year 2000.

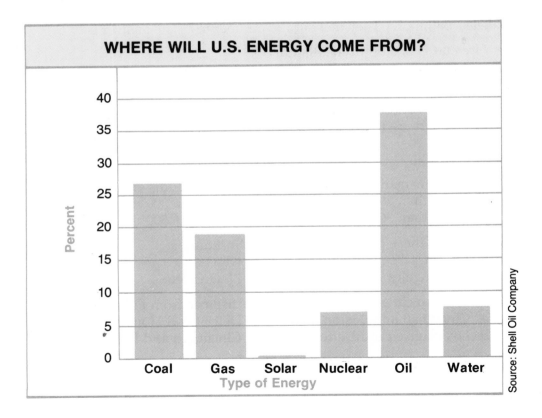

WHERE WILL U.S. ENERGY COME FROM?

Source: Shell Oil Company

A bar graph makes it easy to compare things at a glance. To read the graph, look where each bar ends. Then find the closest number at the side of the graph.

Use the graph on page 160 to answer these questions. Choose the best answer.

1. What percentage of U.S. energy probably will be gas by the year 2000?
   a. 19%
   b. 7%
   c. 38%
   d. 8%

Check your answer. The bar for gas reads about 19%. The answer is **a.**

2. About 7% of U.S. energy will come from __.
   a. nuclear power
   b. solar power
   c. oil
   d. water power

3. What type of energy will the United States probably use the least?
   a. water power
   b. coal
   c. solar power
   d. oil

4. What percentage of energy will be supplied by coal and gas combined?
   a. 15%
   b. 46%
   c. 36%
   d. 20%

5. The percentage of coal used will be about how much greater than the percentage of gas used?
   a. 37.8%
   b. 3%
   c. 19%
   d. 8%

6. The second most-used type of energy probably will be __.
   a. gas
   b. coal
   c. nuclear power
   d. water power

7. The U.S. probably will use twice as much oil as which other type of energy?
   a. coal
   b. water power
   c. gas
   d. nuclear power

8. The percentage of energy supplied by all types of energy, except oil, will probably be __.
   a. more than the amount of oil used
   b. less than the amount of oil used
   c. the same amount
   d. none of the above

Pumping Away

It is the strongest muscle in your body. It is always working. It pumps an average of 1,500 gallons of blood through your body every day. In two years, that amount would fill a million-gallon tank. Even so, we know that your heart still needs just as much exercise as the other muscles in your body need.

Many people jog to exercise their hearts. The line graph below follows the changes in the heart rate of a jogger during a 25-minute period of time.

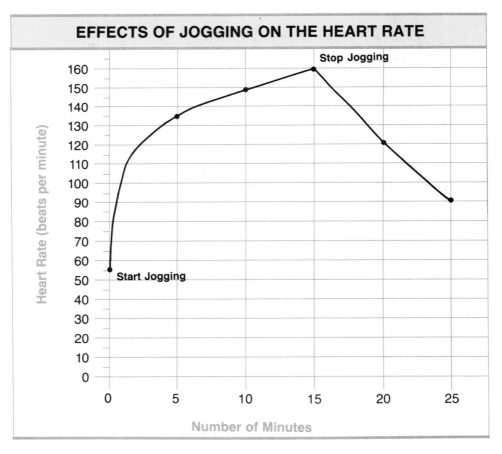

A line graph shows at a glance how something has changed over a period of time. An upward swing in this line shows an increase in the jogger's heart rate. A downward swing shows a decrease in heart rate.

Use the graph on page 162 to answer these questions. Choose the best answer.

1. What was the jogger's heart rate after 5 minutes of jogging?
    a. 135 beats per minute
    b. 55 beats per minute
    c. 150 beats per minute
    d. 5 beats per minute

Check your answer. Find 5 minutes at the bottom of the graph. Look at the dot above it. Now follow the dot across to 135 beats per minute. The answer is **a**.

2. When the jogger started out, what was her heart rate?
    a. 0 beats per minute
    b. 50 beats per minute
    c. 55 beats per minute
    d. 160 beats per minute

3. When was the highest heart rate recorded?
    a. 5 minutes
    b. 15 minutes
    c. 20 minutes
    d. 25 minutes

4. What was the jogger's heart rate 10 minutes after she stopped?
    a. 90 beats per minute
    b. 150 beats per minute
    c. 100 beats per minute
    d. 25 beats per minute

5. How much did the jogger's heart rate increase between 5 and 10 minutes of jogging?
    a. 25 beats per minute
    b. 15 beats per minute
    c. 100 beats per minute
    d. 135 beats per minute

6. What does this line graph show?
    a. The heart rate remained about the same during jogging.
    b. The heart rate decreased slowly during jogging.
    c. The heart rate increased during jogging.
    d. The heart rate increased after the jogger stopped.

7. As the jogger continues to rest, what do you think will happen to her heart rate?
    a. It will increase slightly.
    b. It will decrease to 0 beats per minute.
    c. It will decrease to about 55 beats per minute.
    d. It will stay the same.

Electric Power

Where does your electricity come from? Electricity doesn't just happen because you flip a switch. In some parts of the United States, people get their electricity from water power. If you live in the Northeast, for example, most of your electricity probably comes from dams and waterfalls. This is called hydroelectric power. But if you live in the Midwest, most of your electricity probably is made from coal, gas, or oil. In other parts of the country, nuclear power is sometimes used to make electricity.

Americans use a lot of electricity. The graph below shows how much hydroelectric power and nuclear power were made between 1977 and 1980 in the United States.

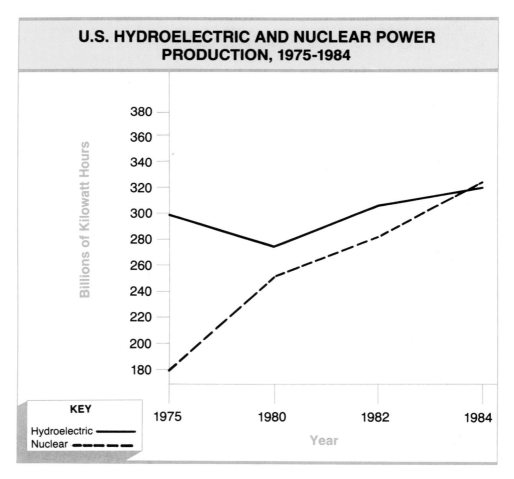

U.S. HYDROELECTRIC AND NUCLEAR POWER PRODUCTION, 1975-1984

Billions of Kilowatt Hours

Year

KEY
Hydroelectric ———
Nuclear ━ ━ ━ ━

Some line graphs have two lines. The key tells you what each line represents. The line graph on page 164 compares U.S. hydroelectric power (water power) with nuclear power production. Electricity is measured in kilowatt hours (kws).

Use the line graph for these questions. Choose the best answer.

1. What year shows the highest production of both hydroelectric power and nuclear power?
   a. 1975
   c. 1982
   b. 1984
   d. 1980

Check your answer. The graph shows the highest point on both lines is 1984. The answer is **b**.

2. About how much hydroelectric power was made in 1982?
   a. 309 billion kws
   c. 325 billion kws
   b. 276 billion kws
   d. 320 billion kws

3. In what year was more nuclear power than hydroelectric power produced?
   a. 1984
   c. 1975
   b. 1982
   d. 1980

4. In which years did nuclear power production increase?
   a. 1975 to 1984
   c. 1974 to 1975
   b. 1975 to 1980
   d. 1984 to 1985

5. How much did nuclear power production rise from 1980 to 1984?
   a. about 70 billion kws
   c. about 100 billion kws
   b. about 40 billion kws
   d. about 11 billion kws

6. The amount of nuclear power made in 1980 was ___.
   a. more than in 1984
   c. the same as 1984
   b. less than in 1984
   d. 0

7. About how much less hydroelectric power than nuclear power was made in 1984?
   a. 120 billion kws
   c. 4 billion kws
   b. 22 billion kws
   d. 174 billion kws

8. Since 1982, what happened to the gap between the amount of nuclear power and hydroelectric power?
   a. It decreased.
   c. It stayed the same.
   b. It increased.
   d. None of the above.

The Water Planet

We call our planet Earth. The ancient Roman people called it Terra, which means "soil" or "earth." But the fact is that our planet is mostly covered with water. No other planet in this solar system has even half as much water. However, there is no chance that we will change the name of our planet. It's a name, you might say, that is firmly planted in the earth.

The graph below shows how much of Earth is water and how much of it is land. The names of the oceans and the continents are on the graph. Study it.

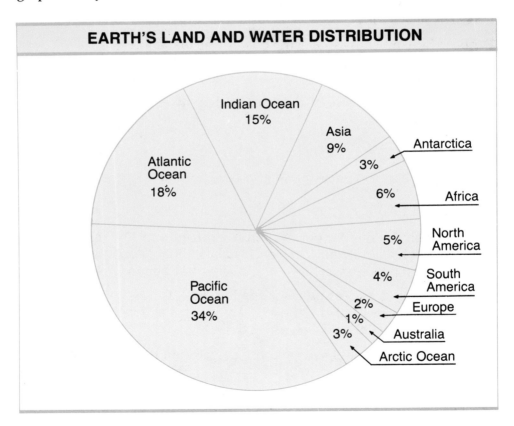

EARTH'S LAND AND WATER DISTRIBUTION

A circle graph shows how a whole is divided into parts. Each part has a number, or a percentage. Together, the parts of the circle add up to 100 percent. By looking at the circle graph of Earth, you can quickly see how the size of each part compares to other parts.

166

Use the graph on page 166 to answer these questions. Choose the best answer.

1. The smallest ocean is the ___.
    a. Indian Ocean   c. Arctic Ocean
    b. Pacific Ocean   d. Atlantic Ocean

Check your answer. Look for the ocean with the smallest percentage. The answer is **c**.

2. Which continent has only 3% of Earth's area?
    a. Antarctica   c. Europe
    b. South America   d. Australia

3. What percentage of land is taken by North America and South America together?
    a. 5%   c. 9%
    b. 4%   d. 30%

4. There are four oceans. What percentage of Earth is covered by water?
    a. 70%   c. 34%
    b. 100%   d. 40%

5. What is the total percentage of land on Earth?
    a. 9%   c. 30%
    b. 50%   d. 100%

6. Which ocean covers a larger area than all the continents put together?
    a. Indian Ocean   c. Pacific Ocean
    b. Arctic Ocean   d. Atlantic Ocean

7. Which of these statements is *not* true?
    a. The Pacific Ocean is the largest ocean on Earth.
    b. Asia is the largest continent on Earth.
    c. Europe is the smallest continent on Earth.
    d. Africa covers more land than South America.

How Many Are We?

It's been done every 10 years since 1790. In that year, the United States Congress passed the Census Act. This law required the government to count *all* the people in the United States. The last census was taken in 1980. A form was mailed to every household in the U.S. on March 28. What did the census find out? It showed that there were over 226 million people living in the United States in 1980.

The graphs below give you information about the population of the U.S. in 1980. Study them.

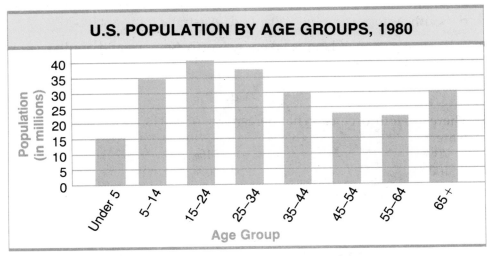

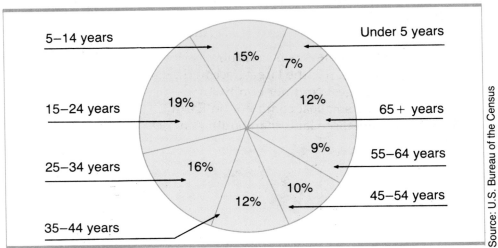

Source: U.S. Bureau of the Census

The circle graph on page 168 shows what percentage of the total population each age group was in 1980. The bar graph shows how many people there were in each age group in 1980. Together, the two graphs give you a good picture of the U.S. population in the year 1980.

Use the graphs to answer these questions. Choose the best answer.

1. Which graph shows how many people there were in 1980 between the ages of 45 and 54?
   a. circle graph
   b. bar graph
   c. both of them
   d. neither of them

Check your answer. The bar graph shows how many people there were in each age group. The answer is **b**.

2. Which age group had the largest percentage of the population in 1980?
   a. under 5 years
   b. 15–24 years
   c. 25–34 years
   d. 65+ years

3. About what percentage of the population was under five years old?
   a. 7%
   b. 17%
   c. 10%
   d. none of the above

4. About how many people were between 5 and 14 years old in 1980?
   a. 42,000,000
   b. 25,000,000
   c. 15,000,000
   d. 35,000,000

5. According to the census, about 25 million people were 65 or older. Which other age group had the same number of people?
   a. under 5 years
   b. 35–44 years
   c. 45–54 years
   d. none of the above

6. About how many more people were 25–34 than were 35–44?
   a. 25 million
   b. 7 million
   c. 37 million
   d. 12 million

7. What percentage of the population was under 15 years old?
   a. 100%
   b. 15%
   c. 22%
   d. 50%

8. Together, the two graphs show that ___.
   a. less than half the population is under 65
   b. less than half the population is over 5
   c. more than half the population is under 35
   d. more than half the population is over 34

Sometimes, tests have questions that use visual materials such as maps, tables, and graphs. Use the visual materials as you follow the test tips on the next four pages. Put your answers on your answer sheet.

Test Tips: Study each map quickly. Look at the map key and the compass rose. Read each question and use the map to answer it. Then check your answer by looking at the answer choices.

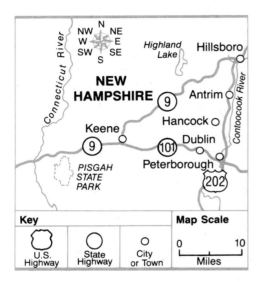

Choose the best answer.

1. In what direction is Keene from Hillsboro?
a. northeast   c. southeast
b. northwest   d. southwest

2. Which highway would you take from Peterborough to Hillsboro? In what direction?
a. 101 south   c. 9 south
b. 202 north   d. 202 south

3. About how far is Dublin from Peterborough?
a. 1 mile   c. 10 miles
b. 5 miles   d. 15 miles

4. North Carolina and South Carolina both produce __.
a. furniture   c. chemicals
b. steel   d. textiles

5. How many states produce paper goods?
a. one   c. three
b. two   d. four

6. Which state makes clothing?
a. North Carolina
b. South Carolina
c. Georgia
d. Florida

COMPARISON TABLE

	U.S.	U.S.S.R
Population	236,423,000	272,500,000
Area (sq. mi.)	3,628,150	8,647,172
Grain Prod. (tons)	177,314,000	98,500,000
TV's in Use	143,000,000	75,000,000
Literacy Rate	99%	99%
Life Expectancy (years)	72 (Male) 76 (female)	63 (male) 72 (female)

U.S. SOFT DRINK MARKET

By Company

Pepsico —25.6%
Coca-Cola— 36.4%
Others— 18.1%
Canada Dry —2.6%
Royal Crown Cos.—3.4%
Dr. Pepper —6.8%
Seven-Up —7.0%

By Product Type

Cola—63.2%
Others—5.3%
Root Beer—4.9%
Orange—7.0%
Lemon-lime—12.7%
Pepper type—6.9%

Choose the best answer.

7. How many square miles does the U.S. have?
   a. 8,647,172   c. 229,800,000
   b. 3,628,150   d. 2,416,000

8. How many more years can a male in the U.S. expect to live than a male in the U.S.S.R.?
   a. 10 years   c. 12 years
   b. 2 years   d. 9 years

9. How many more TV sets are being used in the U.S. than in the U.S.S.R.?
   a. 143 million   c. 218 million
   b. 75 million   d. 68 million

Test Tips: Answer the easier questions first. Then go back and do the harder ones.

10. The two circle graphs show ___.
    a. food consumption
    b. soft drink consumption
    c. cola and uncola taste test results
    d. growth of cola industry

11. What percent of soft drinks are not cola drinks?
    a. 31.1%   c. 5.3%
    b. 11.9%   d. 36.8%

12. Which company produced the largest quantity of soft drinks?
    a. Pepsico
    b. Coca-Cola
    c. Seven-Up
    d. Other

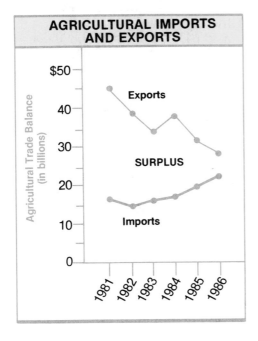

AGRICULTURAL IMPORTS AND EXPORTS

Know what information is on each graph. Check your answers against the graphs.

Choose the best answer.

13. What years show an increase in farm exports?
a. 1983-1984　　c. 1985-1986
b. 1982-1983　　d. 1981-1982

14. What years show the only decrease in farm imports?
a. 1982-1983　　c. 1981-1982
b. 1985-1986　　d. 1983-1984

15. About how much more farm exports were there in 1981 than in 1986?
a. $12,000,000　c. $9,000,000
b. $35,000,000　d. $17,000,000

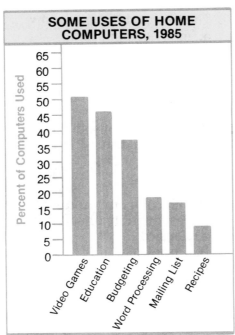

SOME USES OF HOME COMPUTERS, 1985

16. What are most home computers used for?
a. video games
b. word processing
c. recipes
d. education

17. What percentage of home computers are used for budgeting?
a. 16%　　　　c. 37%
b. 51%　　　　d. 18%

18. Next to video games, about 46 percent of home computers are also used for ___.
a. education
b. word processing
c. budgeting
d. mailing lists

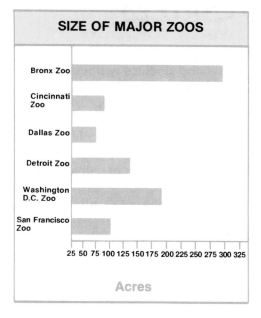

SIZE OF MAJOR ZOOS

Bronx Zoo
Cincinnati Zoo
Dallas Zoo
Detroit Zoo
Washington D.C. Zoo
San Francisco Zoo

25 50 75 100 125 150 175 200 225 250 275 300 325

Acres

Test Tips: Know what is being asked. Focus on the key words in each question.

Choose the best answer.

22. What kind of map would show where emeralds are mined?
    a. street
    b. agriculture
    c. product
    d. weather

23. What would you use to figure out directions on a map?
    a. key
    b. map scale
    c. compass rose
    d. none of the above

24. What kind of map would show were the Lincoln Memorial is?
    a. world
    b. street
    c. weather
    d. product

25. Which of the following would show the exact numbers of video recorders in Japan?
    a. line graph
    b. table or chart
    c. circle graph
    d. bar graph

19. According to the graph, which zoo is the largest?
    a. Bronx Zoo
    b. Dallas Zoo
    c. Detroit Zoo
    d. Cincinnati Zoo

20. Which zoo is almost as large as the Cincinnati Zoo?
    a. Washington D.C. Zoo
    b. Detroit Zoo
    c. Dallas Zoo
    d. Bronx Zoo

21. Where is the zoo with the smallest land area?
    a. Dallas
    b. Cincinnati
    c. Detroit
    d. Washington D.C.

Reference Skills

Are candy bars good for you? Most dentists and doctors will tell you no. Candy bars have sugar as their main ingredient. Doctors urge people to cut down on their sugar by cutting out candy bars.

But candy-makers disagree. They say that less than 8 percent of a person's sugar comes from candy. Besides, a one-ounce chocolate bar has 2.2 grams of protein, as against 1.3 grams for a banana and 0.4 grams for an apple. A chocolate bar also offers 65 grams of calcium, as opposed to 10 and 15 grams for a banana and an apple.

Suppose you wanted to know more about the value of candy bars. You can find all the facts above, and more, in reference materials. There are many different types of sources. These are just a few of them.

A. Dictionary

C. Almanac

B. Encyclopedia

D. Books

E. Newspapers and Magazines

You don't have to read all these references to find the facts you need. You just have to know where to look. Do you know which one to use to find what you need? Test yourself. Answer these questions. Choose the best answer.

1. Which would you use to learn the history of candy-making in the United States?
   a. dictionary   c. encyclopedia
   b. newspaper   d. almanac

2. Which would list the countries that produced the most candy last year?
   a. cookbook   c. encyclopedia
   b. almanac   d. magazine

3. Which would give the ingredients and instructions for making caramel clusters?
   a. encyclopedia   c. cookbook
   b. almanac   d. dictionary

The Yucca

Few plants are as useful as the yucca plant. Yucca plants grow in the southwestern United States and in Mexico. The Indians who lived in those areas found many ways to use the yucca. The leaves can be used to make rope, mats, baskets, and even sandals. The roots and stems are good for making soap. You can also eat the buds and flowers. And when the fruit has been dried, it can be made into a drink. If you don't want to use your yucca plant in these ways, it also has a pretty flower that can be used for decoration.

Yucca is one of the words on the dictionary page below.

yesterday

¹yes·ter·day |yes′·tər·dā | *adv* **1.** On the day last past; on the day preceding today. **2.** At a time not long past; only a short time ago. —**yesterday** *adj*

²yes·ter·day *n* **1.** The day last past; the day before the present day. **2.** Recent time; time not long past. **3.** Past time.

yew |yōō| *n* **1.** Any of a genus of evergreen trees and shrubs with stiff linear leaves and fruits with a fleshy aril. **2.** The wood of a yew.

yip |yĭp| *v* **1.** To bark sharply, quickly, and often continuously. **2.** To utter a short sharp cry. —**yip** *n*

¹yo·del |yōd′ ·ll *v* To sing by changing from a natural voice to a falsetto and back; also to shout or call in a similar manner.

²yo·del *n* A song or refrain sung by yodeling; also a yodeled shout or cry.

yurt

young·ster |yŭng′·stər| *n* **1.a.** A young person; youth; **b.** child; **c.** a person in the relatively early years of life or of a career. **2.** A young mammal, bird, or plant.

yo-yo |yō′ · yō| *n* A thick grooved double disk with a string attached to its center that is made to fall and rise to the hand by unwinding and rewinding on the string.

yuc·ca |yŭk′ əl *n* (from the Spanish) Any of several plants of the lily family, having long, often stiff, leaves on a woody base and bearing a large cluster of white blossoms.

yum·my |yŭm′·ēl *adj Informal* Appetizing; delicious.

yurt |yŏort| *n* (of Turkic origin) A circular domed tent of skins or felt stretched over a collapsible framework; used by the Kirghiz and other Mongol nomads of Siberia.

Pronunciation Key

ă bat/ ā ray/ â dare/ ä dark/ ĕ bet/ ē he/ ĭ dig/ ī die/ î ear/ ŏ hot/ ō so/ ô for/ oi join/oŏ hood/   ōō hoot/ ou out/ ŭ bug/ û fur/ th the/ th thin/ ə ago

Entries in a dictionary are listed alphabetically. Guide words appear at the top of every page. They tell the first and last entries on the page. Each entry shows the syllables, the pronunciation, and the part of speech of the word. Sometimes the dictionary tells what language the word comes from. The meaning or meanings of the word are given.

Use the dictionary sample on page 176 to answer these questions. Choose the best answer.

1. *Yoga* would appear on this page between which two words?
   a. *yew* and *yip*
   c. *yodel* and *youngster*
   b. *yip* and *yodel*
   d. *youngster* and *yo-yo*

Check your answer. The first two letters in *yodel, yoga,* and *youngster* are the same. Look at the third letter in each word. The answer is **c**.

2. Which word would be found on a page before this one?
   a. yield
   c. yen
   b. yet
   d. zany

3. Which of these words has exactly two syllables?
   a. yesterday
   c. yurt
   b. yew
   d. yucca

4. Which word is pronounced like *yew*?
   a. me (mē)
   c. sew (sō)
   b. you (yo͞o)
   d. yet (yĕt)

5. What language does the word *yucca* come from?
   a. Turkish
   c. Russian
   b. Greek
   d. Spanish

6. Which of the following words has more than one meaning?
   a. yesterday
   c. yucca
   b. yo-yo
   d. yurt

7. The word *yip* is sometimes used as a verb and sometimes as a noun. Which other word can be a verb or a noun?
   a. yo-yo
   c. yew
   b. yodel
   d. yummy

8. Which word fits best in the following sentence? The family ate their dinner inside the __.
   a. yucca
   c. yo-yo
   b. yurt
   d. yodel

I'll Trade You

Before there was money, people traded. A visit from the doctor might be paid for with a basket of potatoes. This was called bartering. Today, many people are again bartering to get the things they need. Here's how it might work: An auto mechanic fixes an artist's car. Instead of cash, the artist gives the mechanic a painting. With today's high taxes and inflation, there's a lot to be said for bartering. And lots of people are doing it.

The table of contents and a part of the index from a book on bartering are given below.

THE BARTER BOOK
by Dyanne Asimow Simon

TABLE OF CONTENTS

Chapter	Page
1 An Introduction to Barter	1
2 Barter in the Past	8
3 Individual Barter	17
4 Collective Barter	29
5 The Economics of Barter	52
6 Is Barter for You?	70
7 Some Things To Watch For	81
Bibliography	143
Index	147

Index

Binn, Moreton, 21, 62–63

Computers, in barter, 4, 15, 35, 37, 38, 40, 47

Corporations: barter by, 61–62 overhead of, 59

Exchange Enterprises, 4

Gray Bears, 48

Horsetrading, 14, 17–22, 40–41 rules for, 22 trading up in, 18

International barter, 61–64

Jewelry cooperatives, 121

Trading up. *See* Horsetrading.

A table of contents is found in the front of a book. It lists the chapters of the book and the page each chapter begins on. An index is found in the back of a book. It lists topics in the book alphabetically by key words. It tells what page each topic is found on. A bibliography is sometimes found in the back of a book. It is a list of the sources the author used to get the facts.

Use the table of contents and the part of the index on page 178 to answer these questions. Choose the best answer.

1. Which chapter would tell you about the history of barter?
   a. 1   c. 5
   b. 2   d. 9

Check your answer. History is the study of the past. The answer is **b**.

2. Which pages will give you information on what bartering is?
   a. 1–7   c. 81–142
   b. 29–51   d. 143–146

3. If you want to find out what not to do when you barter, which chapter should you read?
   a. 6   c. 1
   b. 7   d. 4

4. Which chapters would help you find out if you should try bartering?
   a. 2 and 5   c. 2 and 4
   b. 1 and 2   d. 3 and 6

5. Moreton Binn has his own company that arranges trades between different kinds of businesses. Which pages would tell about him?
   a. 21, 62–63   c. 95–98
   b. 14, 17–22   d. 129–142

6. Which page should you turn to in order to find out about trading up?
   a. 14   c. 22
   b. 18   d. 52

7. Suppose you want to find more information about how to barter. On what pages could you find the names of other books on the topic?
   a. 70–80   c. 143–146
   b. 95–112   d. 147–152

Roller Skating

All over the country, people love to roller-skate. People of all ages skate in parks and at skating rinks. Some people skate to music. Some people skate to work. But roller skating did not start out as a sport for everybody. The inventor, James Leonard Plimpton, introduced his "rocking skates" in the 1860's. Plimpton opened roller rinks. He did not sell his skates, but he rented them only to people who were wealthy enough to join his rinks.

Ann-Victoria Phillips wrote a book called *The Complete Book of Roller Skating*. The book's three library catalog cards are given below.

AUTHOR CARD

796.21
P

Phillips, Ann-Victoria
   The Complete Book of Roller Skating

Workman Publishing, 1979

796.21
P

The Complete Book of Roller Skating
Phillips, Ann-Victoria

Workman Publishing, 1979

TITLE CARD

SUBJECT CARD

796.21
P

ROLLER SKATING
Phillips, Ann-Victoria
   The Complete Book of Roller Skating

Workman Publishing, 1979

Books are listed in the card catalog in the library according to author, title, and subject. All three kinds of cards are arranged in drawers in alphabetical order. The number in the upper left corner of the card tells you where to find the book in the library.

Use the catalog cards on page 180 to answer these questions. Choose the best answer.

1. Suppose you know only the name of the book, *The Complete Book of Roller Skating*. You want to find out who wrote it. What letter should you look up in the card catalog?
   a. T
   b. C
   c. R
   d. P

Check your answer. Title cards begin with the first word in the title. When the first word is *the, a,* or *an,* look for the next word. The correct answer is **b.**

2. If you want to find more books by Ann-Victoria Phillips, what would you look up in the card catalog?
   a. Ann-Victoria
   b. Phillips
   c. Roller Skating
   d. Workman

3. If you want to find more information about roller skating, what should you look up?
   a. Ann-Victoria
   b. Phillips
   c. Complete
   d. Roller Skating

4. Where would you look for information about ice skating?
   a. author card
   b. title card
   c. subject card
   d. none of the cards

5. In what year was *The Complete Book of Roller Skating* published?
   a. 796
   b. 1860
   c. 1979
   d. 1982

6. You will find subject cards for books on roller skating in the card catalog drawer marked ___.
   a. Rog–Sab
   b. Pe–Phy
   c. Com–Coo
   d. Sue–Thc

7. To find *The Complete Book of Roller Skating* in the library, you would look between books with the numbers ___.
   a. 300–399
   b. 500–599
   c. 700–799
   d. 800–899

Doctor Computer

A computer working as a doctor? A computer can help diagnose illnesses. It can suggest treatments for illnesses that have been stored in its memory. A computer is also very good at billing people.

Doctors need to know lots of information. Computers can store great amounts of information, and that information can be gotten easily. The question is: How is a computer's bedside manner?

The *Readers' Guide to Periodical Literature* can help you find magazine articles about medical and other uses for computers. Study the sample entry.

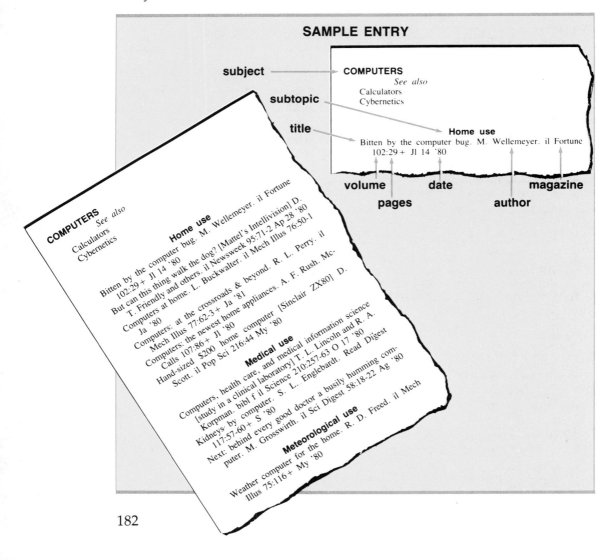

SAMPLE ENTRY

subject — COMPUTERS
  See also
  Calculators
  Cybernetics

subtopic —

title —

Home use

Bitten by the computer bug. M. Wellemeyer. il Fortune 102:29+ Jl 14 '80

volume   date   magazine
    pages   author

COMPUTERS *See also*
Calculators
Cybernetics

Home use

Bitten by the computer bug. M. Wellemeyer. il Fortune 102:29+ Jl 14 '80

But can this thing walk the dog? [Mattel's Intellivision] D. T. Friendly and others. il Newsweek 95:71-2 Ap 28 '80

Computers at home. L. Buckwalter. il Mech Illus 76:50-1 Ja '80

Computers: at the crossroads & beyond. R. L. Perry. il Mech Illus 77:62-3+ Ja '81

Computers: the newest home appliances. A. F. Rush. Mc-Calls 107:86+ Jl '80

Hand-sized $200 home computer [Sinclair ZX80] D. Scott. il Pop Sci 216:44 My '80

Medical use

Computers, health care, and medical information science [study in a clinical laboratory] T. L. Lincoln and R. A. Korpman. bibl f il Science 210:257-63 O 17 '80

Kidneys by computer. S. L. Englebardt. Read Digest 117:57-60+ S '80

Next: behind every good doctor a busily humming computer. M. Grosswirth. il Sci Digest 58:18-22 Ag '80

Meteorological use

Weather computer for the home. R. D. Freed. il Mech Illus 75:116+ My '80

The *Readers' Guide to Periodical Literature* is a reference book that lists magazine articles. Articles are listed alphabetically by subject or author. Each subject entry lists all the articles written on that subject in one year. It names the title, author, magazine, volume number, and pages.

Use the section of the *Readers' Guide* on page 182 to answer these questions. Choose the best answer.

1. The article "Kidneys by Computer" is listed under the subtopic Medical use. Who wrote the article?
   a. T. L. Lincoln   c. S. L. Englebardt
   b. R. A. Korpman   d. M. Grosswirth

Check your answer. The author's name is always listed after the title of an article. The answer is **c**.

2. In which magazine will you find the article "Next: Behind Every Good Doctor a Busily Humming Computer"?
   a. *Scientific American*   c. Grosswirth
   b. *Science Digest*   d. *Reader's Digest*

3. The article "Computers, Health Care, and Medical Information Science" appeared in which issue of *Science* magazine?
   a. October 17, 1980   c. August 1980
   b. September 1980   d. October 1, 1980

4. On what page does the article "Weather Computer for the Home" begin in the May 1980 issue of *Mechanics Illustrated*?
   a. 76   c. 116
   b. 80   d. 1

5. Which article is not listed under the subtopic Home use?
   a. "Bitten by the Computer Bug"
   b. "Weather Computer for the Home"
   c. "Hand-Sized $200 Home Computer"
   d. "But Can This Thing Walk the Dog?"

6. Articles on pocket calculators would be listed under ___.
   a. Computer   c. Mathematics
   b. Calculators   d. Cybernetics

7. The *Readers' Guide* is a series of books. Which book in the *Readers' Guide* would have this section on computers?
   a. 1979–1980   c. 1981–1982
   b. 1980–1981   d. 1982–1983

The Grump

For millions of people in Africa and Asia, life without camels would be unthinkable. Camels are needed for transportation, food, clothing, and energy. For these people, the camel is truly "man's best friend."

Unfortunately, the camel doesn't feel the same way about people. Camels do not like people. They don't even seem to like other camels. In fact, camels don't seem to like much of anything. Unlike dogs or horses, camels do not develop any sense of loyalty to their owners. Given the opportunity, they will bite or kick anyone or anything. They are also known for spitting at people.

Information about camels can be found in an encyclopedia.

INDEX

Cambridge Flag [U.S. history]
Flag (First United States Flags) **F:181** *with picture*
Cambridge Modern History [book by Acton]
Acton, Lord **A:28**
Cambridge Platonists [philosophers]
Plato (Plato's Place in Western Thought) **P:504b**
Cambridge University [England] **C:63** *with picture*
Cambridge **C:62**
Extension Service **E:355**
Great Britain (Education) **G:330e–330f**
Cambyses [Persian ruler]
Iran (The Persian Empire) **I:321**
Persia, Ancient (The Achaemenid Empire) **P:262c**
Camden [New Jersey] **C:63**
New Jersey (Places To Visit) **N:206**
Camden, Battle of [1780]
Revolutionary War in America (table) **R:265;** (The War in the South) **R:267–268**
Came [fine arts]
Stained Glass (Making Stained-Glass Windows) **So:645–646**
Camel [animal] **C:64** *with pictures*
Africa *picture on* **A:119**
Algeria *picture on* **A:344**
Animal (Animals That Help Man) **A:447–448;** (Drought) **A:473;** *picture on* **A:458**
Arab *picture on* **A:546**
Desert **D:131** *with picture;* (Travel in the Desert) **D:132**
Dromedary **D:283**

An encyclopedia is a set of books that gives facts about people, places, and things. Each book is called a volume. The articles in each volume are in alphabetical order. The last volume is usually an index that lists all the topics in the encyclopedia alphabetically. The part of the index on page 184 gives the letter of the volume, followed by the page number for each topic.

Use the information on page 184 to answer these questions. Choose the best answer.

1. In which volume and on what page will you find an article titled "Camel"?
a. A: 119
b. A: 334
c. C: 64
d. D: 131

Check your answer. The article titled "Camel" would be listed in the index under C. The correct answer is **c**.

2. How many volumes have information on camels?
a. one
b. three
c. four
d. five

3. In which volume and on what page would you find a picture of Cambridge University in England?
a. Volume 3, page 62
b. Volume 3, page 63
c. Volume 7, page 181
d. Volume 6, page 355

4. Which volume has information on the Battle of Camden?
a. Volume 2
b. Volume 16
c. Volume 3
d. Volume 4

5. Which would be the best volume to look in to find the sizes of the planets Mercury and Venus?
a. Volume 13
b. Volume 15
c. Volume 17
d. Volume 20

6. "The Star-Spangled Banner" was written by Francis Scott Key. In which two volumes of the encyclopedia would you find information about it?
a. Volumes 7 and 18
b. Volumes 11 and 14
c. Volumes 11 and 17
d. Volumes 11 and 18

LESSON 6

Ballooning

On June 5, 1783, the Montgolfier brothers of France made a hot-air balloon that would carry people. But instead of a person, they sent up a duck. And a rooster. And a sheep! The balloon traveled a mile and a half, and landed eight minutes later. The king was so impressed that he offered the brothers a criminal to use as a guinea pig. However, a man who thought it would be a great honor to make the first balloon flight went instead. The balloon sailed over Paris for about five-and-a-half miles. This flight, too, was a success.

The map below shows where France is located.

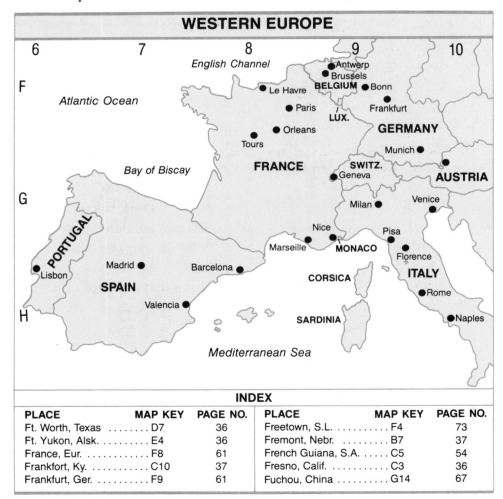

INDEX

PLACE	MAP KEY	PAGE NO.	PLACE	MAP KEY	PAGE NO.
Ft. Worth, Texas	D7	36	Freetown, S.L.	F4	73
Ft. Yukon, Alsk.	E4	36	Fremont, Nebr.	B7	37
France, Eur.	F8	61	French Guiana, S.A.	C5	54
Frankfort, Ky.	C10	37	Fresno, Calif.	C3	36
Frankfurt, Ger.	F9	61	Fuchou, China	G14	67

To find where a certain place is located, check an atlas. An atlas contains maps of many places and tables of geographical facts. To locate a place, first look at the index at the back of an atlas. A section of an atlas index is shown on page 186.

Use the map and index to answer these questions. Choose the best answer.

1. What is the letter/number key used to find France on the map?
    a. E4   c. I8
    b. F8   d. D7

Check your answer. Look at the index listing under France. The map key tells you the letter/number coordinates of France. Look at the map to check the coordinates. The answer is **b**.

2. This map of France can be found on what page of this atlas?
    a. 8   c. 61
    b. F   d. 16

3. The index lists a city in China named Fuchou. On what page will you find a map of Fuchou?
    a. 20   c. 33
    b. 14   d. 67

4. What letter/number key and page number are given for Fremont, Nebraska, in this index?
    a. B7, page 37   c. C5, page 54
    b. B7, page 76   d. F4, page 73

5. What city is located on this map at H10?
    a. Naples   c. Frankfurt
    b. Madrid   d. Paris

6. What is the letter/number key for Milan, Italy, on this map?
    a. C10   c. 61
    b. G9   d. none of the above

Youngest U.S. President

In 1901, Theodore Roosevelt became president of the United States. He was only 42 years old—the youngest president in U.S. history. According to the law, a person must be at least 35 years old to be elected president. More than half of the American presidents have been over 50 years old. And many have even been over 60. Ronald Reagan was 69 years old when he took office in 1981. That made him the oldest person to become president.

Parts of an almanac giving facts about the presidents of the United States are shown below.

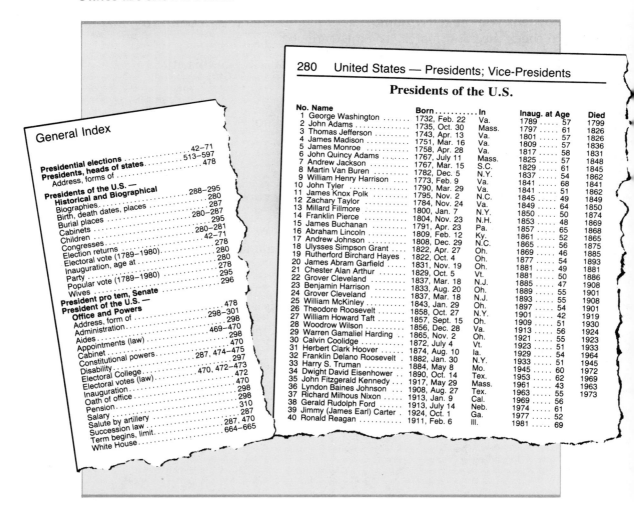

General Index

Presidential elections	42–71
Presidents, heads of states	513–597
Address, forms of	478
Presidents of the U.S. —	
Historical and Biographical	288–295
Biographies	280
Birth, death dates, places	287
Burial places	280–287
Cabinets	295
Children	280–281
Congresses	42–71
Election returns	278
Electoral vote (1789–1980)	280
Inauguration, age at	280
Party	278
Popular vote (1789–1980)	295
Wives	296
President pro tem, Senate	478
President of the U.S. —	
Office and Powers	298–301
Address, form of	298
Administration	469–470
Aides	298
Appointments (law)	470
Cabinet	287, 474–475
Constitutional powers	297
Disability	470, 472–473
Electoral College	472
Electoral votes (law)	470
Inauguration	298
Oath of office	298
Pension	310
Salary	287
Salute by artillery	287, 470
Succession law	664–665
Term begins, limit	
White House	

Presidents of the U.S.

No. Name	Born	In	Inaug. at Age	Died
1 George Washington	1732, Feb. 22	Va.	1789 57	1799
2 John Adams	1735, Oct. 30	Mass.	1797 61	1826
3 Thomas Jefferson	1743, Apr. 13	Va.	1801 57	1826
4 James Madison	1751, Mar. 16	Va.	1809 57	1836
5 James Monroe	1758, Apr. 28	Va.	1817 58	1831
6 John Quincy Adams	1767, July 11	Mass.	1825 57	1848
7 Andrew Jackson	1767, Mar. 15	S.C.	1829 61	1845
8 Martin Van Buren	1782, Dec. 5	N.Y.	1837 54	1862
9 William Henry Harrison	1773, Feb. 9	Va.	1841 68	1841
10 John Tyler	1790, Mar. 29	Va.	1841 51	1862
11 James Knox Polk	1795, Nov. 2	N.C.	1845 49	1849
12 Zachary Taylor	1784, Nov. 24	Va.	1849 64	1850
13 Millard Fillmore	1800, Jan. 7	N.Y.	1850 50	1874
14 Franklin Pierce	1804, Nov. 23	N.H.	1853 48	1869
15 James Buchanan	1791, Apr. 23	Pa.	1857 65	1868
16 Abraham Lincoln	1809, Feb. 12	Ky.	1861 52	1865
17 Andrew Johnson	1808, Dec. 29	N.C.	1865 56	1875
18 Ulysses Simpson Grant	1822, Apr. 27	Oh.	1869 46	1885
19 Rutherford Birchard Hayes	1822, Oct. 4	Oh.	1877 54	1893
20 James Abram Garfield	1831, Nov. 19	Oh.	1881 49	1881
21 Chester Alan Arthur	1829, Oct. 5	Vt.	1881 50	1886
22 Grover Cleveland	1837, Mar. 18	N.J.	1885 47	1908
23 Benjamin Harrison	1833, Aug. 20	Oh.	1889 55	1901
24 Grover Cleveland	1837, Mar. 18	N.J.	1893 55	1908
25 William McKinley	1843, Jan. 29	Oh.	1897 54	1901
26 Theodore Roosevelt	1858, Oct. 27	N.Y.	1901 42	1919
27 William Howard Taft	1857, Sept. 15	Oh.	1909 51	1930
28 Woodrow Wilson	1856, Dec. 28	Va.	1913 56	1924
29 Warren Gamaliel Harding	1865, Nov. 2	Oh.	1921 55	1923
30 Calvin Coolidge	1872, July 4	Vt.	1923 51	1933
31 Herbert Clark Hoover	1874, Aug. 10	Ia.	1929 54	1964
32 Franklin Delano Roosevelt	1882, Jan. 30	N.Y.	1933 51	1945
33 Harry S. Truman	1884, May 8	Mo.	1945 60	1972
34 Dwight David Eisenhower	1890, Oct. 14	Tex.	1953 62	1969
35 John Fitzgerald Kennedy	1917, May 29	Mass.	1961 43	1963
36 Lyndon Baines Johnson	1908, Aug. 27	Tex.	1963 55	1973
37 Richard Milhous Nixon	1913, Jan. 9	Cal.	1969 56	
38 Gerald Rudolph Ford	1913, July 14	Neb.	1974 61	
39 Jimmy (James Earl) Carter	1924, Oct. 1	Ga.	1977 52	
40 Ronald Reagan	1911, Feb. 6	Ill.	1981 69	

An almanac is a reference book that has many facts on both history and current events. A new, up-to-date almanac is written every year. Some almanacs have the index in the front of the book, and others have it in the back. The information in an almanac is very brief. When you need a lot of information, use an encyclopedia or a book on the topic.

Use the parts of the almanac on page 188 to answer these questions. Choose the best answer.

1. To find out what constitutional powers the president of the United States has, under what heading would you look in the index?
   a. Presidents of the U.S. — Historical and Biographical
   b. Presidents, heads of states
   c. President of the U.S. — Office and Powers
   d. Presidential elections

Check your answer. The key words are *President of the U.S.* and *powers.* So the answer is **c.**

2. On which page would you learn what the president's salary is?
   a. 298   c. 288
   b. 310   d. 42

3. On which page would you find the name of President Carter's wife?
   a. 288   c. 478
   b. 899   d. 295

4. Jimmy Carter won the 1976 election, but not by many votes. On which page would you find how many popular votes he got?
   a. 899   c. 278
   b. 280   d. 908

5. According to this almanac, where was President Andrew Jackson born?
   a. North Carolina   c. Virginia
   b. South Carolina   d. Massachusetts

6. Which of the following information would *not* be found on page 298?
   a. the president's salary   c. the president's birthdate
   b. the president's pension   d. names of the president's aides

7. Which of the following probably would *not* appear in any almanac?
   a. population of each state   c. complete history of World War II
   b. names of Olympic winners   d. famous people's birthdates

Different Kinds of Hearing

Deaf people can "hear" in two different ways. They can use sign language or they can lip-read.

There are two articles below about new things that are happening for deaf people. The article on the left is a newspaper article about the use of sign language. The one on the right is a magazine article about a new aid for lip reading.

NEWSPAPER ARTICLE	MAGAZINE ARTICLE

Deaf Will Get Sign Aid At Opera "Susannah"

The New York City Opera will present "Susannah" in a sign-interpreted performance for the deaf Tuesday at 8 p.m.

Two interpreters will be on the left side of the stage. All available front orchestra seats are being held for sale to the hearing-impaired.

The ideas for the performance originated with Ann Silver, consultant for the New York Deaf Cultural Arts Community, and Muffy Greenough, Beverly Sills's daughter, both of whom have been deaf from birth.

Tickets for the performance at $25 are available through the Theater Access Project, Theater Development Fund, 1501 Broadway, New York, NY 10036, or Department H, New York City Opera, Lincoln Center, New York, NY 10023. A synopsis of the opera will be enclosed when the tickets are mailed.

Computerized Glasses For the Deaf!

Why would a deaf person need glasses?

To help him or her read *lips*!

Trying to tell what people are saying just by watching their lip movements can be very confusing. (Try watching a television drama without the sound.)

What sorts of problems do deaf lip readers face? Here are some examples.

The lip position for the sound "he" is *almost* the same as the position that produces the sound "geh" in the word *get*. And there are many more "look-alike" sounds in the English language. That's why two very different statements — like "He can go." and "Get a coat." — actually look alike to a deaf person.

But the National Aeronautics and Space Administration is working along with the Research Triangle Institute of North Carolina to clear up the confusion. They're designing a pair of computerized glasses that "read lips." The computer is programmed to pick up the tricky sounds and to flash a symbol for the sound on the lens of the glasses. And that should take some of the guesswork out of lip reading!

A newspaper article gives very current information. It gives the basic facts by answering the questions who, what, where, when, and why. A magazine article, however, can give more details and more background information. It is not as up-to-date as a newspaper article, but it is more current than a book. Some magazines have articles about just one subject, such as sports or science.

Use the articles on page 190 to answer these questions. Choose the best answer.

1. The newspaper article does *not* tell you ___.
   a. where the opera will be held
   b. what opera is being performed
   c. other things being done for deaf people
   d. where to buy tickets for the opera

Check your answer. A newspaper article gives the basic facts. The correct answer is **c**.

2. The magazine article does not tell you ___.
   a. information on lip-reading problems
   b. where you can buy computerized glasses
   c. who is designing the computerized glasses
   d. how computerized glasses work

3. Where might you find other articles about new glasses for the deaf?
   a. a daily newspaper   c. the card catalog
   b. an almanac   d. the *Readers' Guide*

4. Where would you find the score of last night's ball game?
   a. an almanac   c. a sports magazine
   b. a newspaper   d. a science magazine

5. Where would be the best place to look for facts on the president's new tax plans?
   a. a news magazine   c. an encyclopedia
   b. a history book   d. a science magazine

6. A newspaper would be the best place to look for information on ___.
   a. strike laws   c. yesterday's truck drivers' strike
   b. the history of strikes   d. last year's teachers' strike

7. A magazine would be the best place to look for information on ___.
   a. sales on glasses   c. the invention of eyeglasses
   b. names of eye doctors   d. the newest trends in eye care

191

The Prize

Wilhelm Conrad Röentgen won it in 1901 for his discovery of X rays. Pearl S. Buck won it in 1938 for the books she wrote. Martin Luther King, Jr., won it in 1964 for his work for equal rights for all people. What did they each win? The Nobel Prize.

The first Nobel Prizes were given in 1901. They are awarded to people for their work in the fields of medicine, physics, chemistry, literature, peace, and since 1969, economics. Winning the Nobel Prize is not only a great honor, but also worth about $190,000. The money comes from a fund left by Alfred B. Nobel, the inventor of dynamite.

Left to right: Röentgen, King, Buck. Bottom, center: Nobel, pictured on prize medal named after him.

The facts in the story above did not all come from the same source. Some came from an encyclopedia, some from an almanac, and some from a book about the Nobel Prize. When you write a story based on facts, first decide what facts you need. Then choose the references where the facts are most likely to appear.

Choose the best answer.

1. Which source would most likely tell you who won the Nobel Peace Prize last year?
a. atlas
b. almanac
c. dictionary
d. textbook

Check your answer. The source that gives lots of facts about a particular year is the almanac. The correct answer is **b**.

2. Which source would you use to find out when Alfred B. Nobel lived?
a. dictionary
b. newspaper
c. encyclopedia
d. atlas

3. Alfred Nobel was born in Sweden. The prizes are given out in Sweden each year. Where would you look to find a map of Sweden?
a. newspaper
b. almanac
c. book about Alfred Nobel
d. atlas

4. Where would you look to find a review of a new movie?
a. sports magazine
b. newspaper
c. encyclopedia
d. book

5. Which of these sources would tell you what the word *metamorphosis* means?
a. almanac
b. magazine
c. dictionary
d. atlas

6. Where would you look to find the names of magazine articles about fly fishing?
a. book about fishing
b. encyclopedia
c. newspaper
d. *Readers' Guide*

7. Which source would be most useful to find out about the newest discoveries about clouds?
a. science magazine
b. atlas
c. science textbook
d. almanac

8. Which of these sources would tell you about the Battle of Gettysburg in the Civil War?
a. dictionary
b. history book
c. magazine
d. atlas

Practice your reference skills as you follow the test tips on the next three pages. Put your answers on your answer sheet.

Test Tips: Read each answer choice carefully. Then narrow your choices. Eliminate wrong answers until you are left with the correct answer.

Choose the word that would come first if the four words or names were in alphabetical order.

1. a. roast
b. rinse
c. row
d. refrigerator

2. a. witch
b. wigwam
c. winner
d. wire

3. a. clerk
b. clearance
c. clean
d. clearly

4. a. Anders, Phil
b. Andrews, Steven
c. Andrews, Stephanie
d. Anderson, Kay

Test Tips: Study the reference material shown before you read the questions.

Use the dictionary entry below to answer questions 5–7.

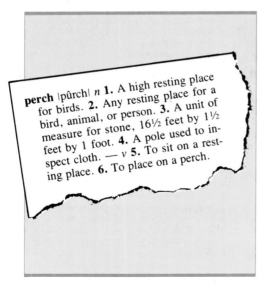

perch |pûrch| *n* **1.** A high resting place for birds. **2.** Any resting place for a bird, animal, or person. **3.** A unit of measure for stone, 16½ feet by 1½ feet by 1 foot. **4.** A pole used to inspect cloth. — *v* **5.** To sit on a resting place. **6.** To place on a perch.

5. How many syllables does the word *perch* have?
a. one   c. three
b. two   d. four

6. Which definitions use the word *perch* as a verb?
a. 3 and 6   c. 1 and 2
b. 5 and 6   d. 4 and 5

7. Which definition of *perch* is used in the following sentence? I perched on the fence to watch the race.
a. 3   c. 5
b. 6   d. 1

Test Tips: Sometimes it helps to use the given reference material to answer the question *before* looking at the answer choices. Then check yourself by finding your answer among the choices.

Here is a table of contents from a book called *Movie Stunts.* Use it to answer questions 8 and 9.

CONTENTS

Chapter	Page
1 The First Stunt People	5
2 Preparing for the Stunt	11
3 Super Stunts	31
4 How They Do It	37
5 Getting Started	45
Index	63

8. Which chapter would tell about the history of stunts?
   a. 1   c. 4
   b. 2   d. 6

9. Which pages would you read to find out how stunts are done?
   a. 45–52   c. 53–60
   b. 5–10   d. 37–44

Use this index from *Wild Foods* to answer questions 10–14.

INDEX

Blueberry, wild, 21, 147
   soup, 150
Cakes, 122–123
Dandelion, 7, 35
   boiled or steamed, 38
   salad, 38–39
Fish, 15
Grape, wild, 21, 159
   jelly, 163–164
Honey, compared to sugar, 166
Jellies, 114–115, 163–164
Mint, wild, 21, 110
   jelly, 114–115
   tea, 114
Poisonous plants, 4, 5, 6, 104,
   128, 155
Salads, 38–39, 90
Soups, 82, 150
Strawberry, wild, 11, 13, 72
   jam, uncooked, 75
Sugar. *See* Honey.
Vegetables, 38, 82, 106

10. What page would tell how to make tea from wild mint?
    a. 13   c. 11
    b. 114   d. 75

11. What page describes two ways to cook dandelions?
    a. 38   c. 35
    b. 7   d. 74

12. What page tells about sugar?
    a. 16   c. 166
    b. 3   d. 74

13. What pages tell about grape jelly?
    a. 6, 155   c. 147–159
    b. 38–39   d. 163–164

14. On what page could you read about blueberry soup?
    a. 16   c. 106
    b. 82   d. 150

Test Tips: Most study skills tests include questions about the purpose of each reference material. Read each question carefully. Be sure to answer what is being asked — not what you think should be asked.

Choose the best answer.

15. Which reference source would give you the most information about the history of airplanes?
    a. almanac
    b. encyclopedia
    c. science textbook
    d. daily newspaper

16. If you were looking for a job, which source would be most helpful?
    a. sports magazine
    b. atlas
    c. index
    d. daily newspaper

17. Where would the chapters of a book be listed?
    a. table of contents
    b. index
    c. dictionary
    d. card catalog

18. Where would you read an article about sky diving?
    a. *Readers' Guide*
    b. almanac
    c. sports magazine
    d. fashion magazine

19. Where would the definition of the word *physiognomy* be found?
    a. dictionary
    b. atlas
    c. card catalog
    d. table of contents

20. Which would show the location of Sweden?
    a. almanac
    b. dictionary
    c. index
    d. atlas

21. In the book *Motorcycles,* which would tell on what page facts on racing could be found?
    a. table of contents
    b. index
    c. card catalog
    d. atlas

22. Where could you find the author of the book *Your Pet*?
    a. card catalog
    b. *Readers' Guide*
    c. atlas
    d. encyclopedia

23. Where would ads for weekend sales of stereos appear?
    a. monthly magazine
    b. index
    c. atlas
    d. Friday's newspaper

24. Which source would name the magazine that printed the article "New Rock Groups"?
    a. almanac
    b. card catalog
    c. *Readers' Guide*
    d. encyclopedia

UNIT IV
TESTS

Test 1

Reading Comprehension   198

Vocabulary   202

Study Skills   205

Test 2

Reading Comprehension   208

Vocabulary   212

Study Skills   215

READING COMPREHENSION

Directions: This test will show how well you understand what you read. Read each passage. Then do the items that follow it. Choose the best answer for each item. On your answer sheet, fill in the space that goes with the answer you choose.

Farmers' markets have brought a touch of rural life to many U.S. cities. City shoppers are buying tomatoes, corn, peaches, beans, and many other fruits and vegetables in the open air.

City farmers' markets are called "tailgate markets" because the crops are sold from the backs of trucks, or the tailgates. Tailgate markets were found in many downtown centers until supermarkets opened in the 1930's. Then farmers began to sell to companies that supplied the main supermarket chains.

Farmers' markets have several advantages for city residents. They are often in several neighborhoods of a city. They display fresh fruits and vegetables from nearby farms, and these are usually sold at lower prices than supermarkets charge.

The markets benefit farmers as well as customers. Farmers can set their own prices and deal directly with customers. The markets give small farmers a place to make money. Farmers who are not making money are likely to sell their land to developers. So, the markets are also helping to save farmland.

---

1. The main customers for farmers' markets are probably __.
a. small farmers
b. local residents
c. supermarket owners
d. developers

2. Which of these items is *not* mentioned in the passage?
a. peaches   c. potatoes
b. tomatoes   d. corn

3. This passage is mainly about the __ of farmers' markets.
a. benefits   c. history
b. problems   d. location

4. Supermarkets would be more likely to offer __ than farmers' markets.
a. lower prices
b. fresher vegetables
c. more convenient locations
d. a wider variety of foods

5. The word *developers* in the last paragraph refers to people who __.
a. become farmers
b. buy land and build on it
c. sell food to supermarkets
d. shop at farmers' markets

Our eyes were fixed on the bushes. We watched for any movement. As we rounded a bend on our monorail, we saw it — a Siberian tiger. This rare and beautiful creature turned its head to stare back at us.

We continued on, and soon we could see some large shapes ahead. Even from a distance, elephants are easy to spot. Coming closer, we could watch and wonder at the great size and power of these giant mammals. It's much better to see wild animals roaming free than to see them locked in small cages. Yet, a trip to India or Nepal is expensive. We didn't have to go that far, however. The animals we saw running free are in a zoo in a large U.S. city.

Zoo managers are trying to create natural habitats to replace the old cages. They want the animals to live happier, more natural lives. And they want people to see the animals in their natural surroundings.

For centuries, people have been locking animals in small cages to be stared at. But fortunately, this is changing. Modern zoos are becoming less like museums and more like living environments. Today, the needs of the animals are considered when their zoo homes are planned.

6. What is a "natural habitat" in a zoo?
   a. a cage with trees
   b. a kind of museum
   c. a place like an animal's native home
   d. a part of India

7. What is the best title for the passage?
   a. "Running Free in Zoos"
   b. "Living in the Wild"
   c. "Creatures Behind Bars"
   d. "A New Home for Tigers"

8. According to the passage, how do modern zoos benefit people?
   a. by making the animals tame
   b. by showing the animals as they normally live
   c. by giving free tickets
   d. by locking up the animals

9. At the beginning of the passage, the authors are ___.
   a. traveling in Nepal
   b. photographing the animals
   c. looking into a tiger's cage
   d. watching the animals from a train

10. In the future, more zoos will probably ___.
    a. build larger cages
    b. create freer environments
    c. collect Siberian tigers
    d. open in large cities

The following is an editorial in a newspaper.

More than 30 states allow television news reports of court trials. The editors support this position. Today's videotape cameras and microphones are so small and silent that there is little chance of distracting anyone. Microphones and television cameras have become commonplace in daily life — in banks, stores, and elsewhere.

Covering trials on television is the best way to inform the public about the court system.

The following letter is a reply to the editorial.

A fair trial just isn't possible when TV cameras are rolling. Judges, jurors, and witnesses *will* be distracted by knowing that they are being taped for broadcast on the local evening news. TV cameras will distract jurors even if the cameras are small and silent. The job that witnesses do will also be affected. Many witnesses will not want to appear in a trial on television.

Let's use the TV cameras for fictional trials, not real ones.

---

11. Which of the following is a statement of fact?
    a. Trials on TV are helpful.
    b. Many states allow TV cameras in courts.
    c. Let's save cameras for fictional trials.
    d. Witnesses will be affected by cameras.

12. Which of the following states the letter-writer's opinion?
    a. Judges are used to cameras.
    b. Many courts allow cameras.
    c. Let's inform the public.
    d. Cameras prevent fair trials.

13. Why are cameras commonplace?
    a. They are seen everywhere.
    b. They are easy to operate.
    c. They are small and silent.
    d. They distract people.

14. The letter differs from the editorial by ___.
    a. presenting facts only
    b. stating a judge's opinion
    c. presenting opinions only
    d. presenting one side of the argument

15. The editorial supports the opinion that cameras won't distract anyone by saying that ___.
    a. they are small and silent
    b. they are out of sight
    c. no one will recognize them
    d. they are used in banks

Read the passage and the answer choices that follow it. Choose the best answer from each numbered group to complete each blank.

The best-known piece of clothing in India and Pakistan is the *sari*, the dress most women __16__. A sari consists of one length of cotton or silk. It comes in an endless variety of colors. The most expensive saris are those with designs of gold and silver and beautiful patterns. Less __17__ saris are made of rough cloth and have no designs.

Women of wealthy families have dozens of saris. Most women, however, have only one or two __18__ saris. These are reserved for holidays and are worn only a few times a year.

The sari extends to the ground like an evening gown. It is five or six yards in length and about 45 inches wide. The sari is __19__ draped around the waist, then brought up under one arm, then passed over the opposite shoulder. The end of the cloth may also be used as a shawl to cover the head. Women wear a blouse with a sari.

Draping a sari over the body is a special art. There are dozens of different ways in which a woman can __20__ the cloth to fit her mood and the occasion. Often, the way in which she wears her sari reveals the area she came from. Women of some areas wear saris of certain colors.

Many women wear another special kind of clothing. This is a two-piece outfit consisting of tight cotton pants and an upper garment, like a long coat, which comes down to the knees. A silk scarf is usually thrown back over the shoulders. Women wear this when they want more freedom of movement than the sari __21__.

These various outfits can be quite smart. But most women in India and Pakistan usually dress much more simply. Their everyday clothes consist of inexpensive ankle-length skirts and blouses made of cotton. The colors are usually __22__ after hundreds of washings.

---

16. a. carry   c. wash
     b. wear   d. repair

17. a. warm   c. known
     b. strong   d. costly

18. a. good   c. blue
     b. lace   d. inexpensive

19. a. soon   c. first
     b. always   d. slowly

20. a. sew   c. wash
     b. arrange   d. cut

21. a. offers   c. shows
     b. means   d. sells

22. a. bright   c. clean
     b. ragged   d. faded

VOCABULARY

Directions: This test will show if you can recognize words that have the same meaning, words that have opposite meanings, and words with several meanings. Mark your answers on your answer sheet.

For Items 1–10, choose the word or phrase that means the same, or almost the same, as each word in dark type.

1. understand the **drawbacks**
   a. ideas
   b. disadvantages
   c. reasons
   d. feelings

2. a lot of **criticism**
   a. people
   b. information
   c. knowledge
   d. complaints

3. **diligence** of the employee
   a. laziness
   b. hard work
   c. salary
   d. smartness

4. **jostled** in a crowd
   a. shoved
   b. lonely
   c. overpopulated
   d. joined

5. comfortable **residence**
   a. chair
   b. attitude
   c. home
   d. manner

6. **massive** boulders
   a. hard
   b. powerful
   c. crumbling
   d. huge

7. horrible **stench**
   a. nightmare
   b. odor
   c. stain
   d. strain

8. **elementary** task
   a. difficult
   b. diligent
   c. simple
   d. incomplete

9. accepted **reluctantly**
   a. carelessly
   b. readily
   c. calmly
   d. unwillingly

10. dangerous **inmates**
   a. feelings
   b. situations
   c. strangers
   d. prisoners

For Items 11–20, choose the word or phrase that means the opposite of each word in dark type.

11. apply makeup
   a. remove
   b. smear
   c. purchase
   d. put on

12. acted **courteously**
   a. politely
   b. impolitely
   c. cautiously
   d. carelessly

13. flourishing business
   a. successful
   b. old
   c. shrinking
   d. dangerous

14. spacious room
   a. messy
   b. neat
   c. cramped
   d. ugly

15. violated a law
   a. passed
   b. went against
   c. canceled
   d. obeyed

16. plentiful supply
   a. large
   b. small
   c. plain
   d. sufficient

17. dismiss a worker
   a. demote
   b. revive
   c. require
   d. hire

18. zany actions
   a. serious
   b. mysterious
   c. insane
   d. dangerous

19. humane treatment
   a. successful
   b. unsuccessful
   c. uncaring
   d. inexperience

20. mistrust someone
   a. encourage
   b. believe in
   c. recognize
   d. appeal to

For Items 21–28, choose the sentence in which the word in dark type means the same as the definition given.

21. people
    a. Three tall **figures** stood at the counter.
    b. My father **figures** the trip will take six hours.
    c. Bookkeepers must keep rows of **figures** straight.

22. hard work
    a. The high jumper failed in her first **effort**.
    b. Training for a long race takes **effort**.
    c. The new novel was the writer's first **effort**.

23. agreement that ends an argument
    a. The Pilgrims established a small **settlement** in Plymouth.
    b. The two sides reached a **settlement** to end the strike.
    c. The woman was awarded a **settlement** of $2 million.

24. create or form something
    a. We **found** a small boat hidden in the reeds.
    b. Good debaters **found** their arguments upon facts.
    c. The businessman decided to **found** a new company.

25. dangerous or serious
    a. The man suffered **severe** injuries in the accident.
    b. He received a **severe** punishment for the crime.
    c. She always wears very **severe** clothing.

26. busy
    a. The company **occupied** six offices in the building.
    b. The Germans **occupied** France during World War II.
    c. His full schedule kept him **occupied** all day.

27. principle or belief
    a. The Lawsons **value** the time they can spend together.
    b. The salesperson said the car's **value** was $3,000.
    c. Being prompt is an important **value** in business.

28. job or work
    a. The woman sought **employment** as a miner.
    b. Sometimes **employment** of force is needed to get things done.
    c. His hobby requires the **employment** of all his free time.

STUDY SKILLS

Directions: This test will show how well you can find and use information from maps, tables, graphs, and reference materials. Read each question. Four answer choices are given, but only one is right. Fill in the space for the best answer on your answer sheet.

OCEANS AND SEAS OF THE WORLD		
Oceans	Area (in sq. miles)	Greatest Depth (in feet)
Pacific Ocean	63,801,000	36,198
Atlantic Ocean	31,830,000	28,374
Indian Ocean	28,356,000	25,344
Arctic Ocean	5,440,000	17,880
Caribbean Sea	970,000	24,720
Mediterranean Sea	969,000	16,896
South China Sea	895,000	15,000
Bering Sea	875,000	15,800
Gulf of Mexico	600,000	12,300
Sea of Okhotsk	590,000	11,070

1. Which city is located on the Pacific Ocean?
   a. Acapulco   c. Tampico
   b. Monterrey   d. Mexico City

2. Oil and gas fields are found along the ___.
   a. east coast   c. Rio Grande
   b. west coast   d. south

3. In which direction is Tampico from the capital city?
   a. northeast   c. southeast
   b. northwest   d. southwest

4. What city is about 250 miles north of Acapulco?
   a. Tampico   c. Nuevo Laredo
   b. Monterrey   d. Mexico City

5. What is the deepest point of the Atlantic Ocean?
   a. 36,198 feet   c. 28,374 feet
   b. 31,830 feet   d. 11,070 feet

6. What is the area in square miles of the Gulf of Mexico?
   a. 21,300   c. 600,000
   b. 590,000   d. 11,070

7. Which sea has the greatest area?
   a. Bering   c. South China
   b. Caribbean   d. Mediterranean

8. Which ocean is not as deep as the Caribbean Sea?
   a. Pacific   c. Atlantic
   b. Indian   d. Arctic

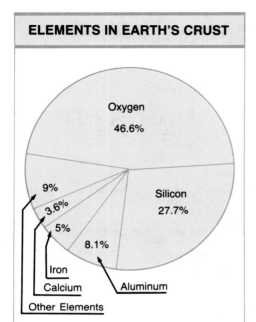

ELEMENTS IN EARTH'S CRUST

Oxygen 46.6%

Silicon 27.7%

9%
3.6%
5%
8.1%

Iron
Calcium
Other Elements
Aluminum

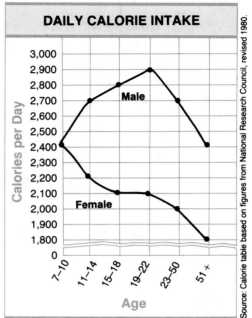

DAILY CALORIE INTAKE

Calories per Day

3,000
2,900
2,800
2,700 — Male
2,600
2,500
2,400
2,300
2,200
2,100
2,000 — Female
1,900
1,800
0

Age: 7–10, 11–14, 15–18, 19–22, 23–50, 51+

Source: Calorie table based on figures from National Research Council, revised 1980.

9. What percentage of the earth's crust is iron?
   a. 50%   c. 46.6%
   b. 5.0%   d. 3.6%

10. Together, silicon and aluminum are what percentage of the earth's crust?
   a. 35.8%   c. 8.1%
   b. 27.7%   d. 46.6%

11. The earth's crust has more iron than ___.
   a. calcium   c. oxygen
   b. aluminum   d. silicon

12. The graph shows that almost half the earth's crust is ___.
   a. iron   c. oxygen
   b. silicon d. aluminum

13. How many calories does an average 30-year-old male need each day?
   a. 2,000   c. 2,100
   b. 2,700   d. 2,200

14. How many more calories does a 13-year-old male need than a 13-year-old female?
   a. 700   c. 2,700
   b. 2,200   d. 500

15. At what age does the average female need the least amount of calories each day?
   a. 11–14   c. 15–18
   b. 23–50   d. 51+

16. Between what ages does the number of calories needed by females stay the same?
   a. 11–18   c. 22–50
   b. 15–22   d. 51+

THE COMPLETE BOOK OF FLYING

Contents

Chapter	Page
Introduction	1
1 Why and How Airplanes Fly . .	6
2 The Nerve Center	41
3 In the Beginning	68
4 Going It All Alone	106
5 Polishing Your Skills	115
6 Highways in the Sky	133
7 Flying After Dark	166
8 The Pilot as Weatherman	176
9 Examination Day	201
10 Mayday! Mayday!	212
11 Keeping Fit To Fly	228

17. How many chapters does *The Complete Book of Flying* have?
a. 228   c. 11
b. 20   d. 1

18. Which chapter probably would tell about the parts of a plane?
a. 3   c. 1
b. 11   d. 6

19. On what page would you begin reading about flying at night?
a. 176   c. 6
b. 212   d. 166

20. Which chapters would tell about learning to fly?
a. 1, 2, 7   c. 2, 4, 8
b. 3, 4, 5   d. 1, 6, 7

Directions: Answer questions 21–25 about reference materials.

21. In which source would you find a review of a new movie?
a. book
b. encyclopedia
c. almanac
d. newspaper

22. Which of these would give the most information on World War II?
a. encyclopedia
b. newspaper
c. atlas
d. almanac

23. Where would you look to find the author of *The Complete Book of Flying*?
a. *Readers' Guide*
b. card catalog
c. encyclopedia
d. almanac

24. In which source would you find the names of all the U.S. vice-presidents?
a. dictionary
b. almanac
c. newspaper
d. atlas

25. Which is the best source for a map showing Kansas?
a. almanac
b. fishing magazine
c. atlas
d. newspaper

Directions: The purpose of this test is to find out how well you understand the materials you read. Read the selection first. Then read each item and decide which answer is correct or clearly better than the others. On your answer sheet, fill in the space that goes with the answer you choose.

Buying toys for small children can be fun, but it's not easy. Always consider a child's level of development when you buy toys. For example, some toys are too advanced for small tots.

Let's start with infants. Everything is new and exciting to children one year old and younger. Bright, shiny mobiles will bring a smile. So will soft, washable dolls, soft rubber balls in bright colors, and nonbreakable objects to chew on. Avoid small toys that can be put into ears, eyes, or mouths, and dolls with button eyes.

A child between one and two years old likes to find out what toys can do. Squeaky toys, squeezable dolls, and stuffed animals are good bets. Blocks and small toys that can be pushed or pulled are also good. Avoid very small toys and toys that have sharp edges.

Toddlers between two and three years old could be called "junior explorers." They will enjoy cars and wagons to push around, kiddie cars, rocking horses, and tip-proof tricycles. This is also a good age for simple musical instruments. Avoid marbles and other small objects.

---

1. The writer's purpose is to __.
   a. give advice on buying toys
   b. recommend certain brands of toys
   c. teach infants how to play
   d. tell a story

2. The writer does *not* discuss __.
   a. the dangers of some toys
   b. electric toys
   c. the best toys for infants
   d. toys with moveable parts

3. One of the writer's main concerns about toys is their __.
   a. size   c. color
   b. shape   d. noise

4. The phrase *junior explorers* in the last paragraph refers to children who __.
   a. enjoy long trips
   b. play with marbles
   c. are active
   d. play an instrument

5. What is the writer's opinion about small toys for children under three years old?
   a. They should be carefully chosen.
   b. They should be colorful.
   c. They should be inexpensive.
   d. They should not be bought.

Scientists have fought a long battle against polio. The disease was known even in ancient Egypt — thousands of years ago.

One of the worst polio epidemics in the United States came in 1916. It affected many people, especially children. Parents worried that their children might die, or be paralyzed for life. In some cities, travel was limited. Children were kept away from crowds.

Today, polio is no longer a feared disease in the U.S. and many other countries. But success in controlling it did not come overnight.

In the 1870's, scientists in Europe found the exact location of the damage caused by the disease. It was in certain cells of the spinal cord. In 1908, a scientist in Vienna, Austria, found that polio was caused by a virus. However, the virus could not actually be seen until the invention of the electron microscope 20 years later. Discovery of the polio virus led to research on making a vaccine.

In 1955, scientists finally found a way to control the disease. Dr. Jonas Salk developed a vaccine and tested it. It was successful. Later, Dr. Albert Sabin developed another vaccine. The vaccines do not cure polio but they help prevent it. The vaccines have made polio a rare disease.

6. The rule to limit travel in 1916 suggests that polio is __.
   a. a disease of ancient times
   b. caused by train travel
   c. easily passed from person to person
   d. caused by a virus

7. Which title describes the main idea of the passage?
   a. "Solving the Polio Puzzle"
   b. "The First Polio Epidemic"
   c. "The Fight Against Disease"
   d. "The Work of Jonas Salk"

8. What step to control polio took place in 1908?
   a. examining cells
   b. finding the cause
   c. discovering a vaccine
   d. curing most cases

9. How is polio prevented?
   a. by seeing a doctor often
   b. by staying away from crowds
   c. by having a vaccination
   d. There is no way of preventing it.

10. The passage suggests that the victory over polio was due to __.
   a. a recent experiment
   b. a scientific miracle
   c. discoveries in the U.S.
   d. many years of research

Francis Bacon, a philosopher and scientist, lived in England in the 1600's. On a snowy day in 1626, he tested his theory that flesh could be preserved by freezing it. He bought a hen, killed it, and stuffed it with snow. The experiment was successful.

Until the early 1900's, no one succeeded in freezing food in large quantities. Efforts to freeze meat in the United States had failed to produce anything that was palatable. But then Charles Birdseye, an explorer and inventor, watched the Inuit tribes freeze caribou meat in the cold, dry air of the Arctic. The meat was still tender and flavorful after it was thawed and cooked months later.

Birdseye realized that the low Arctic temperatures froze the meat much faster than any freezing method that had been tried. He reasoned that quick freezing was essential. He was right. Slow freezing of meat and other foods forms large ice crystals that destroy cell walls. Natural juices leak out when the food is thawed. Faster freezing means smaller ice crystals and better flavor.

Returning to the U.S. with his discovery in 1917, Birdseye formed a company in Massachusetts. The inventor froze everything he could get from the local fishermen — sharks, small whales, even an alligator. After several years of testing, he developed equipment that led to the success of today's huge frozen-food industry.

---

11. Early efforts to freeze meat in the U.S. probably failed because the meat was ___.
a. frozen too fast
b. allowed to thaw
c. not caribou meat
d. frozen too slowly

12. Both Bacon and Birdseye ___.
a. lived in England
b. studied the Inuit tribes
c. formed a company
d. froze animal flesh

13. The word *palatable* in the second paragraph means ___.
a. tasty   c. frozen
b. sweet   d. thawed

14. Which of these harms the taste of meat that has been frozen?
a. moisture
b. dry air
c. low temperatures
d. natural juices

15. Which title best describes the main idea of the selection?
a. "Discovery in the Arctic"
b. "The Early History of Frozen Food"
c. "Charles Birdseye's Invention"
d. "From Tough to Tender"

At the Airport

1 Through the gate, where nowhere and night begin,
2 A hundred suddenly appear and lose
3 Themselves in the hot and crowded waiting room.
4 A hundred others herd up toward the gate,
5 Patiently waiting that the way be opened
6 To nowhere and night, while a voice recites
7 The intermittent litany of numbers
8 And the holy names of distant destinations.

9 None going out can be certain of getting there.
10 None getting there can be certain of being loved
11 Enough. But they are sealed in the silver tube
12 And lifted up to be fed and cosseted,
13 While their upholstered cell of warmth and light
14 Shatters the darkness, neither here nor there.

Howard Nemerov

---

16. In *Line 2*, the phrase *a hundred* refers to __.
   a. passengers waiting to fly
   b. visitors to the airport
   c. passengers getting off a plane
   d. airport workers

17. In *Line 4*, what does the phrase *a hundred others* refer to?
   a. passengers boarding a plane
   b. passengers leaving a plane
   c. the number of planes in the airport
   d. people without tickets

18. The poet seems to believe that a plane ride at night brings a feeling of __.
   a. joy   c. amazement
   b. boredom   d. comfort

19. In *Line 8*, what are the "distant destinations"?
   a. places the passengers have visited
   b. space stations
   c. places where the planes will land
   d. places the poet has visited

20. In *Line 11*, the phrase *the silver tube* refers to __.
   a. a flashlight
   b. an airplane
   c. the wing of an airplane
   d. a silver candlestick

VOCABULARY

Directions: This test will show if you understand the meanings of different words and if you recognize words that have the same meaning. It will also show how well you can use context clues to define new words. Mark your answers on your answer sheet.

For Items 1–10, choose the word or phrase that means the same, or almost the same, as each word in dark type.

1. attractive **attire**
   a. car
   b. home
   c. clothing
   d. offer

2. settle a **dispute**
   a. colony
   b. argument
   c. discussion
   d. plan

3. **proposed** a plan
   a. suggested
   b. rejected
   c. followed
   d. demanded

4. **unruffled** appearance
   a. worried
   b. beautiful
   c. false
   d. calm

5. unbearable **torment**
   a. thought
   b. suffering
   c. action
   d. comment

6. suggested **reforms**
   a. arrangements
   b. changes
   c. reactions
   d. styles

7. scientific **advancements**
   a. experiments
   b. findings
   c. improvements
   d. equipment

8. overcome **adversity**
   a. misfortune
   b. enemies
   c. pain
   d. disturbance

9. **duplicate** a pattern
   a. create
   b. imitate
   c. originate
   d. go against

10. **economic** difficulties
   a. marriage
   b. personal
   c. social
   d. financial

For Items 11–20, read each incomplete sentence. Choose the word or phrase that best completes each sentence.

11. An apprentice learns by serving as an ___.
   a. employer
   b. artist
   c. assistant
   d. actor

12. People take part in recreation for ___.
   a. profit
   b. business
   c. amusement
   d. solving problems

13. Resorts are places to go ___.
   a. on vacation
   b. to find jobs
   c. to make money
   d. to settle arguments

14. An efficient worker is someone who is ___.
   a. slow
   b. lazy
   c. nervous
   d. capable

15. If something is appealing, it is ___.
   a. correct
   b. tempting
   c. unlucky
   d. huge

16. If you are avid about something, you are ___.
   a. unhappy
   b. reluctant
   c. responsible
   d. eager

17. If you show your appreciation to someone, you show ___.
   a. knowledge
   b. gratitude
   c. annoyance
   d. photographs

18. Someone who is dubious about something is ___.
   a. proud
   b. happy
   c. uncertain
   d. strict

19. If clothes are made of durable material, they are ___.
   a. ugly
   b. beautiful
   c. unusual
   d. long-lasting

20. If your income is unlimited, it is ___.
   a. vast
   b. small
   c. undesirable
   d. difficult

For Items 21–26, read the selection below. Notice the words in dark type. Choose the word or phrase that best answers each question about the words in dark type.

In 1912, Native American athlete Jim Thorpe won two gold medals at the Olympic games held in Stockholm, Sweden. He also set two world records. The King of Sweden **proclaimed** to everyone at the games that Thorpe was "the greatest athlete in the world."

However, the next year, Thorpe's records and medals were **withdrawn** from him. They were taken away when it was discovered that Thorpe had been paid for playing baseball during the summer of 1911. Playing for money made Thorpe **ineligible** to participate in the Olympics. Qualified Olympians must be amateurs.

Many people **implored** the leaders of the Olympics to change their decision. They said that Thorpe had not really been a professional athlete. He had earned only a **minute** amount of money playing baseball. In fact, he had been paid a total of only $60 to cover his expenses.

For 70 years, Thorpe's family tried to get the International Olympic Committee to **reverse** its decision. They continued their efforts even after Thorpe died in 1953. Finally, the committee agreed to alter its thinking. In 1982, Jim Thorpe was once again named an Olympic champion.

21. What does **proclaimed** mean in the selection?
   a. thought
   b. believed
   c. announced
   d. wondered

22. What does **withdrawn** mean in the selection?
   a. given
   b. taken away
   c. awarded
   d. pictured

23. What does **ineligible** mean in the selection?
   a. unqualified
   b. qualified
   c. unsuccessful
   d. impossible

24. What does **implored** mean in the selection?
   a. hoped
   b. begged
   c. promised
   d. explored

25. What does **minute** mean in the selection?
   a. timely
   b. free
   c. proper
   d. tiny

26. What does **reverse** mean in the selection?
   a. back up
   b. examine
   c. alter
   d. maintain

Directions: This test will show how well you can find and use information from maps, tables, graphs, and reference materials. Read each question. Four answer choices are given, but only one is right. Fill in the space for the best answer on your answer sheet.

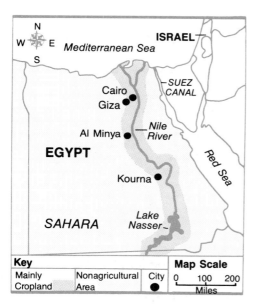

AVERAGE WEIGHT OF AMERICAN WOMEN					
	Age				
Height	20–24	25–29	30–39	40–49	50–59
4'10"	105	110	113	118	121
4'11"	110	112	115	121	125
5'0"	112	114	118	123	127
5'1"	116	119	121	127	131
5'2"	120	121	124	129	133
5'3"	124	125	128	133	137
5'4"	127	128	131	136	141
5'5"	130	132	134	139	144
5'6"	133	134	137	143	147
5'7"	137	138	141	147	152
5'8"	141	142	145	150	156
5'9"	146	148	150	155	159
5'10"	149	150	153	158	162
5'11"	155	156	159	162	166

1. The Nile River is __ of the Red Sea.
   a. east
   b. west
   c. north
   d. south

2. Where are Egypt's croplands?
   a. in the Sahara
   b. around the Nile River
   c. south of Lake Nasser
   d. along the Red Sea

3. Israel is __ of the Suez Canal.
   a. northeast
   b. northwest
   c. southeast
   d. southwest

4. Which city is about 200 miles northwest of Kourna?
   a. Giza
   b. Sahara
   c. Cairo
   d. Al Minya

5. What is the average weight of a 25-year-old woman who is 5'1" tall?
   a. 112 pounds
   b. 114 pounds
   c. 116 pounds
   d. 119 pounds

6. Between the ages of 30 and 40, a 5'5" tall woman will gain an average of __.
   a. 139 pounds
   b. 30 pounds
   c. 134 pounds
   d. 5 pounds

7. On the average, as women get older, their weight __.
   a. increases
   b. decreases
   c. stays the same
   d. none of the above

215

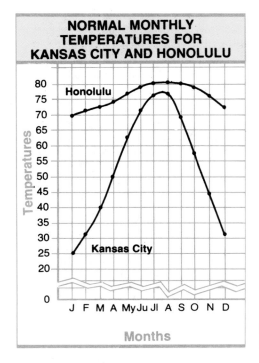

NORMAL MONTHLY TEMPERATURES FOR KANSAS CITY AND HONOLULU

Honolulu

Kansas City

Temperatures

J F M A My Ju Jl A S O N D

Months

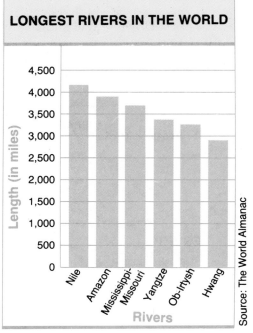

LONGEST RIVERS IN THE WORLD

Length (in miles)

Nile Amazon Mississippi-Missouri Yangtze Ob-Irtysh Hwang

Rivers

8. What is the normal temperature for Honolulu in April?
   a. 70°   c. 55°
   b. 75°   d. 60°

9. How much colder is Kansas City in February than Honolulu?
   a. 10°   c. 72°
   b. 30°   d. 40°

10. Which month is the coldest in Kansas City?
    a. January   c. November
    b. March   d. December

11. During which month is the normal temperature almost the same in both cities?
    a. April   c. September
    b. August   d. November

12. What is the length of the Yangtze River?
    a. 4,100 miles   c. 300 miles
    b. 3,400 miles   d. 10 miles

13. What rivers are longer than the Mississippi-Missouri?
    a. Nile and Hwang
    b. Amazon and Yangtze
    c. Yangtze and Nile
    d. Nile and Amazon

14. How much longer is the Amazon River than the Hwang?
    a. 1,000 miles   c. 2,000 miles
    b. 3,900 miles   d. 100 miles

15. Which river is closest in length to the Ob-Irtysh?
    a. Hwang   c. Yangtze
    b. Amazon   d. Nile

NOW OR NEVER:
The Fight Against Pollution

INDEX

Air pollution, major contributions to,
58–62
Air Pollution Control Association, 47
Cars, smog-control devices in, 163,
171
Clean Air Act, 188
Clean Water Act, 161
Inversion. *See* Temperature inversion;
Smog.
Los Angeles, smog in, 15, 55–56, 62
New York City, deaths from smog in,
46
Photochemical smog. *See* Smog.
Smog: deaths from, 46–47, 188
photochemical, 62
Temperature inversion, 41, 55–56.
See also Smog.

16. On what page would you read about the Clean Water Act?
    a. 47   c. 161
    b. 62   d. 188

17. What page would tell about deaths in New York City from smog?
    a. 46   c. 47
    b. 188   d. 15

18. Facts on photochemical smog can be found on what page?
    a. 46   c. 41
    b. 62   d. 180

19. Which topic would you look under to find out about inversion?
    a. Temperature inversion
    b. Los Angeles
    c. Photochemical smog
    d. Cars

Directions: Answer questions 20–24 about reference materials.

20. Which source would define the word *anthology*?
    a. dictionary
    b. cookbook
    c. almanac
    d. English book

21. In which source would you look for the current population of Vermont?
    a. a book on the U.S.
    b. an almanac
    c. an encyclopedia
    d. a sports magazine

22. Which would give a list of magazine articles on radios?
    a. encyclopedia index
    b. card catalog
    c. *Readers' Guide*
    d. almanac index

23. Where would you look for cookie recipes?
    a. card catalog
    b. almanac
    c. cookbook
    d. encyclopedia

24. A newspaper would be the best source for facts on __.
    a. yesterday's election
    b. Paul Revere's ride
    c. last year's rainfall
    d. Elvis Presley's life

Vocabulary Glossary

Here are all the new words you learned in the vocabulary lessons and their meanings. Remember, sometimes a word can have more than one meaning. The meanings listed here fit the way the words were used in the stories you read.

accustomed — used
acute — sharp or strong
adhere — stick or follow
advancements — improvements
advantageous — helpful
adversity — bad luck or misfortune
affordable — able to be bought
affords — provides
appealing — tempting
apply — put on
appreciation — gratitude
artificial — man-made or not natural
associates — companions
assume — take charge of
asylums — homes for the insane
attire — clothing
attracted — lured or appealed to
attraction — lure or appeal
avid — eager

banned — not allowed
blaze — open up or explore

calculated — measured
canceled — called off
capacity — volume or fullness
competitive — decided by a contest
consult — discuss
continuously — constantly
courteously — politely
craft — art

criticism — complaints
currency — money

dangled — hung
decrease — reduce
dedication — devotion
degree — level or amount
diligence — hard work
dimension — measurement or size
discrimination — prejudice
dismiss — fire or release
dispute — argument
distribute — spread
disturbed — bothered
doubtful — uncertain
drawbacks — disadvantages
dubious — doubtful
duplicate — imitate or copy
durable — long-lasting

economic — financial or money
efficient — capable or skillful
effort — hard work
elementary — simple
eligible — qualified
eliminated — removed
emerged — came out
employment — work
enable — make possible
endorsed — approved
evidence — proof
exceptional — extraordinary
expansion — growth or enlargement

218

fad — popular hobby
federal — national
figures — people
flourishing — growing or thriving
forfeit — give up or lose
formidable — difficult
founded — formed or created
frayed — strained

gracious — charming
guarantee — promise

hasten — hurry
heightened — increased
homeowners — people who
  own houses
hospitality — kindness
humane — caring

illustrate — draw or paint
impolite — rude or not polite
import — bring in
improper — incorrect
inexperienced — untrained or new
injustice — unfairness or
  wrongness
inmates — prisoners
institutions — public buildings
intact — whole or undamaged
interfere — get in the way

jostled — shoved or pushed

manage — control or handle
manufactured — made or
  produced
marathon — long contest
massaged — rubbed
massive — huge
maximum — highest possible
mindful — aware
minted — coined or made

misjudge — guess incorrectly
mistrust — be suspicious of
mounts — horses
mutilated — torn

navigate — guide

obligation — duty
occupied — covered or filled
oppose — go against
outsiders — strangers
overpopulated — overcrowded

partial — part or incomplete
penalty — punishment
plentiful — large or many
popularity — favor or appeal
producer — manufacturer or
  maker
promoted — advanced in rank
proposed — suggested

quantity — amount

recreation — amusement or fun
redeem — trade in or exchange
reforms — changes or
  improvements
regulations — rules
reluctantly — unwillingly or
  unhappily
residence — home
resorts — vacation places
retirees — people who have
  retired
revive — bring back to life
rigorous — difficult

scores — many or lots
settlement — agreement
severe — serious

spacious — open or large
spectators — viewers
stench — odor

techniques — methods
thrive — grow or succeed
throb — pound or beat
tireless — untiring
torment — pain or suffering
treatment — cure or process

unlawfully — illegally

unlimited — vast or endless
unruffled — calm
unsatisfactory — not desirable

value — principle or belief
violated — disobeyed
visualize — see or picture
vocation — job

weather — endure or bear

zany — funny or crazy

Answer Key

UNIT I   READING COMPREHENSION

Pages 14–15: 1. b, 2. c, 3. d, 4. c, 5. d, 6. a

Pages 16–17: 1. c, 2. d, 3. b, 4. b, 5. a, 6. b, 7. c

Pages 18–19: 1. a, 2. d, 3. b, 4. b, 5. d, 6. c

Pages 20–21: 1. c, 2. a, 3. b, 4. c, 5. d, 6. b

Pages 22–23: 1. c, 2. c, 3. a, 4. d, 5. b, 6. c

Pages 24–25: 1. a, 2. c, 3. b, 4. c, 5. d, 6. b

Page 26: 1. a, 2. d, 3. b, 4. c

Page 27: 5. c, 6. b, 7. d, 8. c, 9. b

Page 28: 10. a, 11. c, 12. c, 13. d, 14. b

Page 29: 15. b, 16. a, 17. c, 18. d, 19. b, 20. c

Pages 36–37: 1. c, 2. b, 3. a, 4. c, 5. d, 6. b

Pages 38–39: 1. b, 2. c, 3. b, 4. d, 5. b, 6. a

Pages 40–41: 1. c, 2. a, 3. b, 4. d, 5. a, 6. c, 7. b

Pages 42–43: 1. c, 2. b, 3. a, 4. b, 5. a, 6. d

Pages 44–45: 1. a, 2. b, 3. b, 4. c, 5. d, 6. c

Pages 46–47: 1. b, 2. b, 3. a, 4. c, 5. c, 6. a

Pages 48–49: 1. d, 2. c, 3. c, 4. b, 5. b, 6. a

Pages 50–51: 1. b, 2. d, 3. a, 4. b, 5. d, 6. c, 7. c

Pages 52–53: 1. d, 2. b, 3. c, 4. d, 5. a, 6. b

Pages 54–56: 1. b, 2. a, 3. c, 4. c, 5. d, 6. c, 7. b, 8. c

Page 57: 1. d, 2. b, 3. b, 4. a

Page 58: 5. c, 6. d, 7. b, 8. b, 9. a

Page 59: 10. c, 11. b, 12. d, 13. a, 14. c, 15. d, 16. c

Pages 66–67: 1. b, 2. c, 3. a, 4. d, 5. b, 6. d

Pages 68–69: 1. d, 2. c, 3. a, 4. b, 5. a, 6. c

Pages 70–71: 1. a, 2. b, 3. d, 4. c, 5. c

Pages 72–73: 1. c, 2. d, 3. a, 4. b, 5. b, 6. d

Pages 74–76: 1. c, 2. b, 3. d, 4. a, 5. d, 6. c, 7. a, 8. d

Page 77: 1. c, 2. d, 3. b, 4. a

Page 78: 5. b, 6. a, 7. c, 8. d, 9. b

UNIT II   VOCABULARY

Pages 84 – 85: **A.** 1. competitive, 2. regulations, 3. promoted, 4. endorsed, 5. maximum, 6. interfere, 7. adhere, 8. obligation; **B.** 1. b, 2. c, 3. a, 4. c

Pages 86–87: **A.** 1. emerged, 2. calculated, 3. capacity, 4. proposed, 5. continuously, 6. quantity, 7. visualize, 8. massive; **B.** 1. c, 2. a, 3. b, 4. a

Pages 88–89: **A.** 1. torment, 2. acute, 3. treatment, 4. decrease, 5. throb, 6. accustomed, 7. consult, 8. dangled; **B.** 1. b, 2. c, 3. b, 4. a

Pages 90–91: **A.** 1. federal, 2. minted, 3. mutilated, 4. duplicate, 5. redeem, 6. manufactured, 7. intact, 8. currency; **B.** 1. a, 2. b, 3. c, 4. c

Pages 92–94: **A.** 1. canceled, 2. hospitality, 3. recreation, 4. thrive, 5. attire, 6. founded, 7. employment, 8. economic, 9. attracted, 10. disturbed; **B.** 1. a, 2. c, 3. b, 4. c

Page 95: 1. obligation, 2. adhere, 3. visualize, 4. calculated, 5. torment, 6. decrease, 7. duplicate, 8. mutilated, 9. founded, 10. thrive

UNIT II   VOCABULARY (Concluded)

Pages 98–99:   **A.** 1. settlement, 2. oppose, 3. improper, 4. dispute, 5. violated, 6. unlawfully, 7. injustice, 8. forfeit; **B.** 1. b, 2. a, 3. b, 4. c

Pages 100–101:   **A.** 1. tireless, 2. exceptional, 3. gracious, 4. appreciation, 5. reluctantly, 6. efficient, 7. unruffled, 8. unlimited; **B.** 1. c, 2. a, 3. b, 4. c

Pages 102–104:   **A.** 1. dubious, 2. diligence, 3. appealing, 4. courteously, 5. adversity, 6. inexperienced, 7. formidable, 8. flourishing, 9. impolite, 10. criticism; **B.** 1. b, 2. a, 3. c, 4. b, 5. b, 6. a

Page 105:   1. arguments, agreements, 2. disobeyed, obeyed, 3. go against, favor, 4. extraordinary, ordinary, 5. calm, nervous, 6. thankfulness, ingratitude, 7. energetic, exhausted, 8. untrained, expert, 9. growing, withering, 10. politely, rudely

Page 106:   1. a, 2. c, 3. d, 4. b, 5. d, 6. a, 7. a, 8. b, 9. d, 10. c

Page 107:   11. d, 12. b, 13. a, 14. d, 15. b, 16. c, 17. a, 18. d, 19. a, 20. c

Page 108:   21. b, 22. d, 23. a, 24. c, 25. a, 26. b, 27. a, 28. d, 29. d, 30. c

Page 109:   31. b, 32. b, 33. b, 34. a, 35. c, 36. b, 37. a, 38. d, 39. a, 40. d

Pages 114–115:   **A.** 1. c, 2. a, 3. b, 4. b, 5. a, 6. c, 7. a, 8. c; **B.** fad — popular hobby, marathon — long contest, zany — funny, spectators — viewers, eliminated — removed, penalty — punishment, jostled — shoved, frayed — strained

Pages 116–117:   **A.** 1. b, 2. c, 3. a, 4. c, 5. b, 6. c, 7. a, 8. c; **B.** artificial — not natural, durable — long-lasting, avid — eager, resorts — vacation places, guarantee — promise, techniques — methods, distribute — spread, drawbacks — disadvantages

Pages 118–119:   **A.** 1. c, 2. a, 3. b, 4. c, 5. b, 6. b, 7. c, 8. c; **B.** vocation — job, severe — serious, hasten — hurry, navigate — guide, revive — bring back to life, massaged — rubbed, rigorous — difficult, eligible — qualified

Pages 120–121:   **A.** 1. a, 2. b, 3. b, 4. c, 5. a, 6. c, 7. a, 8. c; **B.** inmates — prisoners, stench — odor, reforms — changes, asylums — homes for the insane, institutions — public buildings, banned — not allowed, unsatisfactory — not desirable, humane — caring

Pages 122:   1. fad, 2. spectators, 3. eliminated, 4. durable, 5. guarantee, 6. hasten, 7. revive, 8. eligible, 9. reforms, 10. humane

Page 123:   1. c, 2. b, 3. a, 4. b, 5. d, 6. d, 7. a, 8. b, 9. d, 10. c

Page 124:   11. b, 12. d, 13. c, 14. a, 15. d, 16. c, 17. a, 18. b

Page 125:   19. a, 20. c, 21. d, 22. b, 23. d, 24. b

Pages 130–131:   **A.** 1. a, 2. b, 3. b, 4. a, 5. b, 6. b, 7. a, 8. a; **B.** 1. illustrate, 2. elementary, 3. affords, 4. craft

Pages 132–133:   **A.** 1. b, 2. a, 3. b, 4. a, 5. a, 6. a, 7. b, 8. a; **B.** 1. discrimination, 2. manage, 3. associates, 4. figures

Pages 134–135:   **A.** 1. a, 2. b, 3. b, 4. b, 5. a, 6. a, 7. b, 8. a, 9. a, 10. b; **B.** 1. dedication, 2. degree, 3. value, 4. dismiss

Page 136:   1. dimension, 2. illustrate, 3. effort, 4. blaze, 5. associates, 6. residences, 7. import, 8. dedication, 9. dismiss, 10. evidence

Page 137:   1. b, 2. c, 3. a, 4. b, 5. b, 6. a, 7. c, 8. a

Pages 142–143:   **A.** 1. c, 2. a, 3. b, 4. b, 5. c, 6. a, 7. c, 8. b

Pages 144–145:   **A.** 1. b, 2. a, 3. c, 4. b, 5. b, 6. a, 7. b, 8. a, 9. b, 10. c

Page 146:   1. d, 2. b, 3. a, 4. c, 5. b, 6. c, 7. d, 8. c

UNIT III   STUDY SKILLS

Page 149:   1. c, 2. b, 3. d, 4. a
Page 151:   1. b, 2. a, 3. c, 4. a, 5. c,
6. c, 7. a, 8. b
Page 153:   1. a, 2. b, 3. d, 4. c, 5. a,
6. d, 7. a
Page 155:   1. a, 2. c, 3. c, 4. c, 5. d,
6. c, 7. a, 8. b
Page 157:   1. b, 2. a, 3. b, 4. b, 5. c,
6. b, 7. a, 8. a
Page 159:   1. c, 2. a, 3. d, 4. b, 5. b,
6. d, 7. b, 8. d
Page 161:   1. a, 2. a, 3. c, 4. b, 5. d,
6. b, 7. c, 8. a
Page 163:   1. a, 2. c, 3. b, 4. a, 5. b,
6. c, 7. c
Page 165:   1. b, 2. a, 3. a, 4. a, 5. a,
6. b, 7. c, 8. a
Page 167:   1. c, 2. a, 3. c, 4. a, 5. c,
6. c, 7. c
Page 169:   1. b, 2. b, 3. a, 4. d, 5. b,
6. b, 7. c, 8. c
Page 170:   1. d, 2. b, 3. b, 4. d, 5. c, 6. b
Page 171:   7. b, 8. d, 9. d, 10. b,
11. d, 12. b
Page 172:   13. a, 14. c, 15. d, 16. a,
17. c, 18. a
Page 173:   19. a, 20. c, 21. a, 22. c,
23. c, 24. b, 25. b
Page 175:   1. c, 2. b, 3. c
Page 177:   1. c, 2. c, 3. d, 4. b, 5. d,
6. a, 7. b, 8. b
Page 179:   1. b, 2. a, 3. b, 4. d, 5. a,
6. b, 7. c
Page 181:   1. b, 2. b, 3. d, 4. c, 5. c,
6. a, 7. c
Page 183:   1. c, 2. b, 3. a, 4. c, 5. b,
6. b, 7. b
Page 185:   1. c, 2. b, 3. b, 4. b, 5. b, 6. d
Page 187:   1. b, 2. c, 3. d, 4. a, 5. a, 6. b
Page 189:   1. c, 2. a, 3. d, 4. c, 5. b,
6. c, 7. c
Page 191:   1. c, 2. b, 3. d, 4. b, 5. a,
6. c, 7. d
Page 193:   1. b, 2. c, 3. d, 4. b, 5. c,
6. d, 7. a, 8. b
Page 194:   1. d, 2. b, 3. c, 4. a, 5. a,
6. b, 7. c
Page 195:   8. a, 9. d, 10. b, 11. a,
12. c, 13. d, 14. d
Page 196:   15. b, 16. d, 17. a, 18. c,
19. a, 20. d, 21. b, 22. a, 23. d, 24. c

UNIT IV   TESTS

TEST 1
Reading Comprehension (pages 198–201):   1. b, 2. c, 3. a, 4. d, 5. b, 6. c, 7. a,
8. b, 9. d, 10. b, 11. b, 12. d, 13. a, 14. c, 15. a, 16. b, 17. d, 18. a, 19. c,
20. b, 21. a, 22. d
Vocabulary (pages 202–204):   1. b, 2. d, 3. b, 4. a, 5. c, 6. d, 7. b, 8. c, 9. d,
10. d, 11. a, 12. b, 13. c, 14. c, 15. d, 16. b, 17. d, 18. a, 19. c, 20. b, 21. a,
22. b, 23. b, 24. c, 25. a, 26. c, 27. c, 28. a
Study Skills (pages 205–207):   1. a, 2. a, 3. a, 4. d, 5. c, 6. c, 7. b, 8. d, 9. b,
10. a, 11. a, 12. c, 13. b, 14. d, 15. d, 16. b, 17. c, 18. c, 19. d, 20. b, 21. d,
22. a, 23. b, 24. b, 25. c

TEST 2
Reading Comprehension (pages 208–211):   1. a, 2. b, 3. a, 4. c, 5. d, 6. c, 7. a,
8. b, 9. c, 10. d, 11. d, 12. d, 13. a, 14. a, 15. b, 16. c, 17. a, 18. d, 19. c, 20. b
Vocabulary (pages 212–214):   1. c, 2. b, 3. a, 4. d, 5. b, 6. b, 7. c, 8. a, 9. b,
10. d, 11. c, 12. c, 13. a, 14. d, 15. b, 16. d, 17. b, 18. c, 19. d, 20. a, 21. c,
22. b, 23. a, 24. b, 25. d, 26. c
Study Skills (pages 215–217):   1. b, 2. b, 3. a, 4. d, 5. d, 6. d, 7. a, 8. b, 9. d,
10. a, 11. b, 12. b, 13. d, 14. a, 15. c, 16. c, 17. a, 18. b, 19. a, 20. a, 21. b,
22. c, 23. c, 24. a

Art Credits: 12, 84, 90–91, Marc Yankus • 14, 66, 80, Frederick Porter • 62, 81, 82, 100, 112, 113, Andrea Baruffi • 78, 96, 103, Tom Lulevich

Photo Credits: 5, IBM • 7, Rosemarie Hausherr • 8, American Airlines • 10, Sara Krulwich/The New York Times • 18, H. Armstrong Roberts • 25, Rocky Weldon/ Leo deWys • 30, Jim Tuten • 32, Picturemakers, Inc. • 36, Neal Boenzi/The New York Times • 39, Robert Rattner • 42, United Press International • 45, The Peregrine Fund/ Laboratory of Ornithology, Cornell University • 46, Ted Lau/Time Inc.; Diagram: Renee Klein/Time Inc. • 49, Paul O. Boisvert • 51, Wide World Photos • 52, Museum of the City of New York • 54, Culver Pictures, Inc. • 68, Children's Television Workshop • 74, *left*, Courtesy of Temple University Office of Public Information; *right*, NBC/TV • 79, Rose-marie Hausherr • 88, Lynn Sugarman • 93, United Press International • 110, Physicians News Service, Inc. • 126, *left*, H. Armstrong Roberts; *center*, Dan Nelken; *right*, H. Armstrong Roberts • 128, General Motors Corp. • 130, Marty Heitner/Taurus Photos • 132, Culver Pictures, Inc. • 138, *left*, Robert A. Isaacs/Photo Researchers, Inc.; *right*, United Press International • 139, The Bettmann Archive • 147, Karri Vinton/Scholastic Photo Awards 1980 • 174, 175, 176, 184, James Gilmour • 192, *left and top center*, Photo Researchers, Inc.; *right*, Culver Pictures, Inc.; *bottom center*, Zenith Radio Corporation

Photo Research: Monique Haimes

Cartography: 148, 150, 152, 154, 156, 170, 186, 205, 215, Graphic Map and Chart Company

Cover Illustration: Jeanette Adams

Cover Photo: Robert Burroughs